Time and the Other

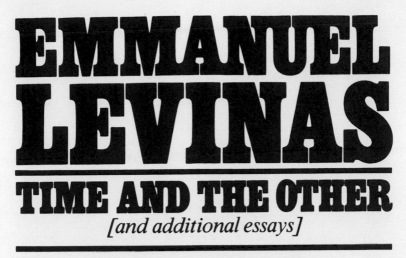

EMMANUEL LEVINAS

TIME AND THE OTHER
[and additional essays]

Translation by Richard A. Cohen

DUQUESNE UNIVERSITY PRESS
Pittsburgh, Pennsylvania

Time and the Other originally appeared as "Le temps et l'autre" in J. Wahl, *Le Choix, Le Monde, L'Existence* (Grenoble-Paris: Arthaud, 1947) it was republished with a new Preface by Levinas in 1979 as *Le temps et l'autre,* copyright 1979 by Fata Morgana, St. Clement, France.

"Diachrony and Representation" first appeared as "Diachronie et représentation," in "University of Ottawa Quarterly," Vol. 55, No. 4, 1985. "The Old and the New" first appeared in a collection entitled *L'Ancien et le nouveau* published by Editions du Cerf, Paris, 1982.

Published in the United States of America
by Duquesne University Press
600 Forbes Avenue, Pittsburgh, PA 15282

Library of Congress Cataloging-in-Publication Data

Lévinas, Emmanuel.
  Time and the other.

  Translation of: Le temps et l'autre.
  Bibliography: p.
  Includes index.
  1. Time. 2. Ontology. I. Title.
B2430.L483T4613 1987 115 87-6900

ISBN 0-8207-0233-1 (paper)

Sixth Printing - November 1995

Contents

Translator's Note   *vii*

Translator's Introduction   *1*

Preface (1979)   29

PART I: 39

    The Solitude of Existing   42
    Existing without Existents   44
    Hypostasis   51
    Solitude and Hypostasis   54
    Solitude and Materiality   55

PART II: 58

    Everyday Life and Salvation   58
    Salvation through the World—Nourishments   62
    The Transcendence of Light and Reason   64

PART III: 67

    Work   68
    Suffering and Death   68
    Death and the Future   71
    The Event and the Other   74
    Other and the Other   77
    Time and the Other   79

PART IV: 80

    Power and Relationship
      with the Other   81
    Eros   84
    Fecundity   90

OTHER ESSAYS   95

    "Diachrony and Representation"   97
    "The Old and the New"   121

Selected Bibliography   139

Index   143

Translator's Note

Time and the Other [*Le temps et l'autre*] was first delivered as a series of four lectures in 1946/47 in Paris at the Philosophical College founded by Jean Wahl. It was published in 1948 in a collection entitled *Choice, World, Existence* [*Le Choix - Le Monde - L'Existence*] (Grenoble-Paris: Arthaud, 1947; pp. 125-196), along with essays by Jeanne Hersh, Alphonse de Waelhens, and Jean Wahl (see Preface footnote 2), who also lectured at the Philosophical College. In 1979 it reappeared, with a new preface, as a separate volume (Montpellier: Fata Morgana).

"The Old and the New" [*L'Ancien et le nouveau*] was delivered as one lecture of a year long lecture series of the same title, given by various authors, offered in 1979/80 at the Catholic Institute of Paris, for masters students in theology. It was published in 1982, along with all the other lectures of that series, in a collection entitled *The Old and the New* [*L'Ancien et le nouveau*], edited by Joseph Doré (Paris: Editions du Cerf; pp. 23-37).

"Diachrony and Representation" [*Diachronie et representation*] was also delivered as a lecture, on October 20, 1983, at the University of Ottawa, on the first day of a three day conference dedicated to Paul Ricoeur, entitled "In Search of Meaning." It was published in the *University of Ottawa Quarterly* (volume 55, number 4, 1985; pp. 85-98), edited by Theodore-F. Geraets. The final three sections, with minor revisions and additions, were also given as a lecture by Levinas on September 2, 1986, at the last session of a ten day colloquium devoted to his thought, entitled "Emmanuel Levinas: Ethics and First Philosophy," held at Cerisy la Salle in Normandy, France, organized by Jean Greisch and Jacques Rolland for the International Cultural Center of Cerisy-la-Salle.

Following accepted conventions in translating Levinas, I have consistently translated the key terms *autrui* and *autre* by "Other" with a capital "O" and "other" with a small "o." (When *Autre* appears capitalized, usually in contrast to the term *Même*, "Same," I show the French original in brackets.) As indicated below (in Preface footnote 3), *autrui* refers to the personal other, the other person, and *autre* refers to otherness in general, to alterity. Still, it must be said, Levinas often uses *autre* where he could very well have used *autrui*; one should avoid making a fetish of this distinction and pay attention to context, though I have kept to the above convention for the sake of consistency.

I have translated *autre homme* as "other person," since the generic sense of "man," which Levinas intends, loses something in the literal translation, "other man." I mention this less to evade potential gender criticisms (see footnote 69), than to steer the reader away from interpreting the expression "other person" as perhaps indicating a shift from the level of subjectivity to the level of personality, which it does not. The text is strewn with the terms "man" and "he," which I have left intact and which are also intended, I believe, in the generic sense of "humankind" and "one."

Levinas' own notes are always preceded by his name, "Levinas:"; all other notes are my own.

Time and the Other recently appeared in German translation: *Die Zeit und der Andere*, translated by Professor Ludwig Wenzler (Hamburg: Felix Meiner Verlag, 1984). I mention this to draw the reader's attention to the Postface by Professor Wenzler, *"Zeit als Nahe des Abwesenden"* ["Time as the Nearness of the Absent"] (*ZA* 67-92), which Levinas has told me he very much admires.

I would like to thank Professor Theodore-F. Geraets, of the University of Ottawa, for sending me a copy of Levinas' manuscript of "Diachrony and Representation," prior to its publication in the *University of Ottawa Quarterly*; Professor André Prévos, of the Pennsylvania State University, Scranton Campus, for painstakingly reviewing with me an earlier version of the translation of *Time and the Other*; Mr. John Dowds, Director of the Duquesne University Press, for the steady support he and the Duquesne University Press have given to this and other Levinas projects; and Loyola College of Maryland for a summer research grant.

Finally, I would like to thank, however inadequately, Professor Emmanuel Levinas, for having given me permission to translate and join together the three texts which make up this volume, and for having conceived them in the first place.

Translator's Introduction

Time and the Other has a genetic phenomenological structure. It begins with existence without existents, describes the origination of the distinct existent, the subject, then moves to the progressively more complex constitutive layers of subjectivity, its materiality and solitude, its insertion in the world, its labor and representation, its suffering and mortality, to conclude with the subject's encounter with the other person, dealt with specifically in terms of eros, voluptuosity and fecundity. Unlike the Hegelian phenomenology, however, these stages mark a progression toward alterity rather than toward totality; they are driven by a desire to break out of the circuits of sameness rather than a yearning for complete comprehension. Thus the analyses begin with what so lacks alterity that it is anonymous like the night itself, existence without existents, what Levinas calls the "there is," and end with what is so radically and irreducibly other that it is the very paradigm of alterity, what Levinas in *Time and the Other* calls the "mystery" of the other person.

The comparison and contrast with the Hegelian phenomenology that Levinas' design recalls is instructive. For both, the end bears on the beginning. For Hegel, the end provides the truth of the beginning. Notions such as "being," "nonbeing," and "becoming," with which Hegel's phenomenology begins, are inadequate and surpassed because they are insufficiently articulate to account for the complex reality whose truth the Hegelian quest seeks to express. These broad and basic terms trip on themselves because they want to express more than they can. Only the fully articulate and absolutely self-reflective Concept, wholly realized at the end of the phenomenological voyage, can adequately say what thought all along was trying to say, yet was all along only saying partially, only stumbling toward, and which is finally said in all its purity in Hegel's *Logic:* the absolute all-inclusive truth. The contrast between Levinas' and Hegel's phenomenology does not result solely from the former adhering to Husserlian phenomenology (the attempt to faithfully describe the origin and constitution of reality in all its manifold and interrelated layers of meaning, without presuppositions). Just as Hegel's phenomenology is driven by a yearning for the total truth, the truth which knows all and knows itself to know all, Levinas' phenomenology is driven by a desire for an exteriority which remains irreducibly exterior, therefore it aims for a liberation from rather than the realization of totality, unity, and the self-same. Levinas' itinerary is not a reverse Hegelianism, ending in indeterminate being; for in Levinas, too, the "end" which moves the "beginning" becomes increasingly complex, determinate, and meaningful. But the end in Levinas is neither an end, a finality, nor a truth, a comprehension. Levinas' thought ends with what has no end: alterity, the infinite, the wholly other. Thus it breaks with Hegelian phenomenology as well as with the noetic-noematic confines of Husserlian phenomenology.

Levinas' itinerary in *Time and the Other*—from anonymous existence to the emergence of subjectivity, to subjectivity's practice, theory and mortality, to its shattering relationship with the alterity of the other person—is essentially the same itinerary as that found in Levinas' immediately preceding work, except that *Existence and Existents* (1947) concludes with a section entitled "On the Way to

Time," and *Time and the Other* (1948) progresses a few steps
further in that very direction. The repetition and difference
expressed in the relationship between these two texts, the
way the analyses of *Time and the Other* retrieve and overlap
the analyses of *Existence and Existents*, and push them a bit
further along, is indicative of the remarkable continuity ex-
hibited by the development of Levinas' thought as a whole.
The movement of Levinas' thought is like that of waves, as
Derrida was the first to say, but we must think of the waves
as those of an approaching high tide: each wave pushing a
bit further than the last, each venturing a more radical interpretation of alterity. Each wave becomes visible dis-
creetly, looms larger and then crashes at the always
turbulent forefront of Levinas' thought.

The design of the two early texts is again followed after
Section I of Levinas' first major work, *Totality and Infinity*
(1961). There the stages spread out in the early works are
brought into an even closer focus; they are far more complex and nuanced; and in some instances they are altered.
Totality and Infinity is a mature work, and again progresses
further toward alterity, now into the choppy domain of ethics, into the infinite obligations and responsibilities of social
life. Levinas' second major work, *Otherwise than Being or
Beyond Essence* (1974), represents the next wave after *Totality
and Infinity,* pushing Levinas' conception of the other person's radical and irreducible alterity into the domain of language, into the Saying which disrupts and gives sense to
the Said. Finally, a recent collection, entitled *God Who
Comes to the Idea* (1982), as well as the article "Diachrony
and Representation," included in this edition of *Time and
the Other*, brings the Other's alterity into relationship with
the absolute alterity of God.

Thus, to summarize and simplify this development, to
describe these oncoming waves with single words, Levinas'
thought progresses through analyses of the alterity of existence in *Existence and Existents;* of time in *Time and the Other;*

of ethics in *Totality and Infinity;* of language in *Otherwise than Being or Beyond Essence;* and of God in *God Who Comes to the Idea* and "Diachrony and Representation." Just as in each work one sees a development from sameness to the alterity which disrupts sameness, in Levinas' work as a whole one sees a progressive radicalization of the sense of the otherness of the other person.

Time and the Other (and *Existence and Existents,* for that matter), then, provides an early but lasting sketch of Levinas' mature thought, and thus affords a clear, bare bones vision of its initial stages.

The summary above is not meant to imply that Levinas dealt with time once and for all in *Time and the Other.* Rather, because Levinas binds time to alterity, the theory of time articulated in *Time and the Other* marks but one moment in a progressively radicalized theory of time that unfolds in Levinas' work as a whole. Each of Levinas' works presents a distinct analysis of time, and each analysis is progressively more radical than the prior analysis, as the analysis of alterity is progressively radicalized.

"The Old and the New" (1982) and "Diachrony and Representation" (1985) represent a return to the theory of time first developed in *Time and the Other.* The important difference, however, is that in these articles the meaning of time is deepened in the light of Levinas' more mature reflections on subjectivity, ethics, language, and God. Beginning with *Existence and Existents,* then, a work very close to *Time and the Other* in chronology and content, it is possible to begin tracing the progressive "alterization" of time as it unfolds across the development of Levinas' entire work. This is the route I will follow in this Introduction.

Existence

In *Existence and Existents* Levinas is concerned primarily with the time of the solitary subject, beginning with the time of the emergent existent: the instant. Following

Bergson's lead, Levinas rejects the classical, abstract, representational theory of the instant. In classical thought, he argues, an abstract time frame, a formal time "line," spreading out into infinite "befores" and infinite "afters" is conceived first, and instants are afterwards placed within it, as its content, each instant being the same as all the others, and each excluding all the others. Levinas retains the idea that instants exclude one another, are separate, monadic, but contrary to the classical theory he conceives the instant concretely, as the very "accomplishment of existence" (*EE* 76). That is to say, he conceives of the instant as originary sensation or materiality. This is the instant Husserl names the *"Urimpression,"* though, he admits, "names are lacking for it." It is an originary self-sensing, where the sensing and the sensed are one and the same, yet are nonetheless, paradoxically, noncoincident.

Levinas thus describes the instant, not in terms of knowledge and causality, which was the error of classical thought, but in terms of existential "conquest"—the subject's escape from anonymous existence—and existential "fatigue"—the subject inescapably burdened with itself, weighed down by its own materiality. "What is absolute in the relationship between existence and an existent, in an instant," he writes, "consists in the mastery the existent exercises on existence, but also in the weight of existence on the existent" (*EE* 77). This early notion of the atomic instant, caught up within itself, mired in itself, in the movement of an inescapable and instantaneous "hypermateriality," will remain throughout Levinas' thought, later playing a crucial role in accounting for the subject's relationship with alterity, the role of the subject's extreme *passivity.*

Time

The instant is again found in *Time and the Other* (Part I). Once again, Levinas characterizes the emergence of subjec-

tivity in terms of its hypermateriality, its intimate and paradoxical self-relationship, its noncoincident self-sensing.
But he also takes up, critically, another sort of time, which
he began to analyze in the concluding sections of *Existence
and Existents*, namely, ecstatic time, Heideggerian temporality. Already, at the end of *Existence and Existents*, Levinas
began to speak of time in terms of an escape from subjectivity, subjectivity's desire to get out of itself, to rid itself of itself, to "save" itself from the mastery and burden of its
material self-relationship as a distinct existent. The instant
has no past or future, it is fragile, evanescent, worldless,
and thus sees in the past and future, in the horizons of the
world, in the dialectic of temporal horizons, an exit from itself. But already, proleptically, in *Existence and Existents*
Levinas wrote of this horizontal escape: "If time is not the
illusion of a movement, pawing the ground, then the absolute alterity of another instant cannot be found in the subject, who is definitively *himself*. This alterity comes to me
only from the other." Instead of seeking alterity in the
world, as Heidegger does, Levinas asks, in the next sentence: "Is not sociality something more than the source of
our representation of time: is it not time itself?... The dialectic of time is the very dialectic of the relationship with
the other, that is, a dialogue which in turn has to be studied
in terms other than those of the dialectic of the solitary subject" (*EE* 93). Of course, this is the very line of study
Levinas does pursue, connecting time to the alterity of the
other person, and progressively radicalizing the sense of
the Other's alterity. But in *Time and the Other*, under the influence of Heidegger's brilliant analyses of being-in-the-
world, this venture toward the Other's alterity passes
though a necessary detour: time as a *relative* rather than an
absolute escape from the immanence of subjectivity. That is
to say, Levinas examines the time of ecstasis and the time of
representation. Thus a later wave, the time of the other person, already appears on the horizon of worldly time, ecstatic temporality.

To characterize time solely in terms of the subject's originary self-relationship, the materiality of the instant, with
its self-mastery and fatigue, is insufficient because the subject is not only mired in itself, an island unto itself, but is
also ecstatically projected into the world. Inasmuch as
Levinas has already caught sight of the subject's desire to
escape itself, in *Time and the Other* the subject's ecstatic projection into the world is characterized as "salvation." The
subject saves itself from its intimate self-enclosure, evades
itself, by being-in-the-world, "loosening the bond between
the self and the ego" (*TO* 00). But in this early work Levinas
is already dissatisfied with Heidegger's interpretation of
the subject's ecstasis in terms of praxis, the use of tools, the
instrumentality of the "in-order-to" (Heidegger's *das Um-
zu*), for he finds that the subject is first *nourished* by the
world, first *enjoys* the world, before using it. Enjoyment is
prior to practice and theory. The relevant point, from the
point of view of time, is that the subject is not merely enclosed within itself, encased within its sensations, in the
self-movement of the sensuous instant, but extends out
into the *horizons* of future and past, horizons opened by the
world and light. But for Levinas, being-in-the-world,
whether in the ecstases of enjoyment, labor, or knowledge,
does not truly break the immanence of subjectivity. The
subject always only finds *itself*, its enjoyment, its labor, its
knowledge, in the ecstatic movement which seems to offer
the promise of an escape outside of itself. Heidegger is per-
fectly clear that the "in-order-to," the referential totality of
the world, ultimately refers back to *Dasein*. Ecstatic time de-
lays rather than disrupts the time of subjectivity; it is a
postponement of immediacy rather than a deposition of
immanence. For Levinas it is insufficiently other.

But such a claim forces Levinas into confrontation with
the great moment of alterity in the Heideggerian ecstatic
theory of time, namely, being-toward-death. What opens
up the horizons of temporality, the horizons of the future
and past, in the Heidegger of *Being and Time*, is ultimately

death. The referential totality of the world ultimately refers back to *Dasein*, but *Dasein* is the being who dies. Death in turn is understood as the "impossibility of possibility" which makes possibilities possible by making them the possibilities of a finite subject, making them the subject's ownmost possibilities, its projection as a being destined to die. How can Levinas claim that ecstatic time is merely a *relative* escape from immanence rather than an *absolute* break from immanence, when precisely death seems to shatter the subject's immanence absolutely? The question is not intended to lead back into the classical tradition which overlooked death, or which took death to be a fall, a punishment or a failure, but of properly interpreting the essential mortality of finite being. Levinas is struck not so much by the *alterity* of death in the Heideggerian analysis, as by its *mineness (Jemeinigkeit)*. Death, for Heidegger, is not only *my own*, it is that which is precisely *most my own*, my *uttermost possibility* of being. It does not shatter *Dasein* but shatter's *Dasein's inauthentic* possibilities. Death individualizes *Dasein*, makes *Dasein* truly be its being. For Levinas, on the other hand, death is not my own, not therefore the "possibility of impossibility," as Heidegger would have it, but the "impossibility of possibility" (*TO* 70n.43). That is to say, against what Levinas describes as the "supreme lucidity and . . . supreme virility" of Heideggerian being-toward-death, *Dasein's* resoluteness, its courage to be, Levinas proposes instead that we recognize another moment, the emasculation and suffering which death brings to subjectivity. He writes: "Death in Heidegger is an event of freedom, whereas for me the subject seems to reach the limit of the possible in suffering. It finds itself enchained, overwhelmed, and in some way passive" (*TO* 70-71).

Levinas, then, in *Time and the Other*, sees in death and mortality not the uttermost possibility of subjectivity, but a countermovement against subjectivity. And in this countermovement, rather than in the Heideggerian projection, he finds time. The future is not what comes from out of me in my being-toward-death, in the resoluteness of my futural projection, but what comes *at* me, ungraspable, outside my possibilities, not as the mastery of death but as the very *mystery* of the death which always comes to take me against my will, too soon.

Death escapes the subject not because the subject flees into a superficial everyday existence, into avoidance and in-authenticity, but because the futurity of death, its unfore-seeability, its ungraspability, overwhelms the subject's powers. "The fact that it deserts every present is not due to our evasion of death and to an unpardonable diversion at the supreme hour," Levinas writes, "but to the fact that death is *ungraspable,* that it marks the end of the subject's virility and heroism" (*TO* 71-72). Such a relationship with an alterity outside my possibilities, is a relationship with a future which can in no way be reduced to self-presence. Furthermore, this future, which is not on my horizon but comes toward it, "indicates," Levinas writes, "that we are in relation with something that is absolutely other, some-thing bearing alterity not as a provisional determination we can assimilate through enjoyment, but as something whose very existence is made of alterity. My solitude is thus not confirmed by death but broken by it" (*TO* 74). That being whose very existence is made of alterity is, of course, the other person. Thus Levinas discovers the alterity of the future not in death as a possibility, which is insufficiently other to escape the subject's self-presence, and is even the very dynamism, the very courage, resoluteness, or mastery of self-presence, but in death as *mystery,* and mystery as the alterity of the other person. Thus *Time and the Other* con-cludes with an examination of the "mystery" of the other person.

In *Time and the Other* Levinas has not yet interpreted so-cial life in the ethical terms he later introduces in *Totality and Infinity.* The time of alterity is situated concretely—a technique Levinas always uses but never fully explains—in terms of the relationship with the Other encountered erotically, in the voluptuosity of the caress that caresses what withdraws and escapes presence, the "feminine Other." Such a relationship goes so far into alterity as to be finally—in a finality without end—in relation with another Other, the child, engendered in fecundity. To mark the extraordinary and irreparable rupture in being that such a relation effects, Levinas calls it "transubstantiation." At this stage of his thought, the erotic relationship (which returns again at the conclusion of *Totality and Infinity*) serves as the "prototype" of the encounter with the radical alterity of the other person. It therefore also serves as the concrete situation wherein time occurs.

One notices in *Time and the Other* that Levinas analyzes only the future of time: "voluptuousness is the very event of the future," he writes, "the future purified of all content, the very mystery of the future." The erotic relationship between the caress and the withdrawal of the feminine, which constitututes the voluptuosity of eros, the acuity of its duality, constitutes time as a relationship with a future that escapes presence absolutely, the Other's future. This emphasis on the future, to the apparent exclusion of the past, figures quite strongly in Levinas' early works. Perhaps, one might think, it indicates a residual Heideggerian influence, the priority of the future over the equiprimordial dimensions of past and present, an influence which Levinas will later shake off. For the later works tend to emphasize the past, almost to the exclusion of the future. Perhaps, too, one might think, this shift indicates the different orientations of Levinas' youth and his age, one looking forward, the other looking back. But such suggestions seem facile, and in any event explain very little. Jacques Rolland is closer to the mark when he argues—with regard to the transition from *Totality and Infinity* to *Otherwise than Being or Beyond Essence*—that there is a movement in Levinas'

thought from a focus on the radical and overwhelming alterity of the Other to a focus on the effect of that alterity on
the subjectivity of the subject. Such a movement, in terms
of time, would account for the early almost exclusive emphasis on the future and the later almost exclusive emphasis on the past, as we shall see. This suggestion is not
intended to fault Levinas. Levinas' emphases are not exclu-
sions. The radical future of *Time and the Other* will require
the radical past of the later works.

The essential point is that time must be conceived in its
full dimensionality. Indeed, precisely what Levinas is attempting to come to grips with, along with Heidegger and
the classical tradition, is the way time *breaks up* reality into
the dimensions of past, present, and future. The problem,
however, is how to characterize the alterity that keeps this
break up—time—open. In rejecting purely conceptual solutions to this problem, Levinas, like all of his contempo-
raries, was quite early influenced by the work of Bergson
(whose major works he acknowledges at the end of "Diachrony and Representation," and whose thought he the-
matizes and criticizes in "The Old and the New"). Neither
can the influence of Husserl and Heidegger, with whom
Levinas studied in the late twenties, be underestimated in
accounting for his rejection of purely conceptual solutions
to the problem of time.

One of Levinas' earliest philosophical labors, in 1935,
was the little known translation of an article by a Russian
thinker, N. Khersonsky, entitled "The Notion of Time." The
Khersonsky article essentially reproduces the Bergsonian
critique of the classical conceptualization of time, its spa-
tialization and abstraction. The cognitive, judgemental,
representation of time is rejected because "the act of judge-
ment's own logical force consists precisely in not separat-
ing the subject and the predicate by time, but in attributing
simultaneity to them both." The time of knowledge is
simultaneity, contemporaneousness. Concrete "living

time," to the contrary, the translation continues, "flows from one instant to another without delaying with any one of them." Throughout the development of his thought, Levinas will always adhere to the critical perspective of this early position, characterizing the time of representation as the time of simultaneity, the contemporaneity of subject and predicate. Levinas does not, however, affirm Bergsonian *duration*—the continual creation of novelty—as a satisfactory alternative to abstract time. The newness of duration is insufficiently opened by otherness, is still too much a product of consciousness, albeit an intuitive consciousness.

For Levinas, the classical conception cannot account for the "fact"—which is the core of Levinas' own theory of time—that the other person encountered face-to-face is not the subject's contemporary, that they do not meet one another "at the same time." The time of the Other and my time, or the times of mineness, ecstatic temporalities, do not occur at the same time. Veritable time, in Levinas' sense, is the effect or event of the disjointed conjunction of these two different times: the time of the Other disrupts or interrupts my temporality. It is this upset, this insertion of the Other's time into mine, that establishes the alterity of veritable time, which is neither the Other's time nor mine.

The problem with time classically conceived has to do with the limitations of *negation* (cf. *TI* 40-43). Approaching time from the point of view of judgemental knowledge, the ancients characterized time's break up of reality in terms of predicative negation: the future and past are *not* present, thus in some sense they *are not*. Caught within the logic of such a perspective, the perspective of propositional judgemental truth, the classical tradition was led inevitably to sacrifice time, as nonbeing, to eternity, first by means of external negations, where only the pure unity of being is affirmed, and finally, with Hegel, by means of internal negations, where an historically evolved unity of being is affirmed. But the whole of contemporary philosophy, and certainly not Levinas alone, rebels against this cognitive reduction of plurality to unity, of nonbeing to being, of time to eternity. This rebellion defines and sets the tasks of the contemporary epoch of thought, and thus again points out the central importance of time. For Levinas the universal categories of being and nothingness are inadequate when it comes to time.

Heidegger, following Husserl, but with much more consistency than Husserl, also rejects the classical tradition and its representational model of knowledge and time. But for Levinas, as we have seen, Heideggerian temporality, while not sacrificing time to the abstract and unified present of propositional knowledge, nonetheless sacrifices time to the ecstatic self-presence of an existential or ontological unity, to the prepredicative fore-structure of understanding. The problem, one must always keep in mind, is how to account for rather than reduce the break up of reality that time effects. The late Heideggerian "thought of Being" means to be Being's thought, but it cannot escape the ablative, the thinker's thought about Being. Heideggerian temporality, for Levinas, does not go far enough. Levinas, more than any other contemporary thinker, insists on the radical alterity of time's dimensions. To do so, as has been indicated, he binds time to the alterity of the other person. Time is neither an abstract difference, in contrast to identity, the obliteration of alterity; nor the concrete identity of difference and identity, the integration of alterity, totalization; but the *non-in-difference* of one person to another, the proximity of the Other, an infinite distance without distance.

Ethics

Thus in *Totality and Infinity* Levinas realizes that binding time to the irreducible alterity of the other person, to the

non-in-difference of one to another, means insisting on an
alterity beyond the identifications effected by both epistemology and ontology. Epistemology and ontology
(whether pre-critical, critical, dialectical, or hermeneuti-
cal), he argues, reduce the alterity of time to the sameness
of the present or presence. The irreducible alterity beyond
the identifications of both epistemology and ontology, thus
beyond truth and reality, the non-in-difference of one to
another, he realizes, is an *ethical* alterity, the alterity of the
good encountered in the face of the Other. Levinas is fond of
recalling, in this regard, Plato's words, "the Good beyond
Being," among other similar formulations in the history of
Western thought, to lend a sort of philosophical dignity to
this so apparently anti-philosophical notion, the notion of a
thought beyond being and truth, the notion of a relation
where the terms related remain absolutely separate yet in
relation.

Recognizing the ethical dimension of alterity, and thus
the inextricably ethical character of the alterity constitutive
of time, means Levinas can no longer remain content to understand, as he did in his earlier works, the rupture time
effects as the "ungraspable," the "unknowable," "mystery,"
or as erotic "withdrawal" and fecund "transubstantiation."
These characterizations of alterity, though not incorrect, express only its negativity, giving pride of place, as it were, to
grasping and knowledge. They begin, however, in precisely the way philosophy has always insisted one *must* always begin, in the beginning, with what has or seeks
beginnings, origins, principles. Philosophy always begins
at the beginning, with knowledge and understanding,
with being and truth, because philosophy has hitherto
been synonymous with first philosophy, with the firstness
of first philosophy as the very *telos* of philosophy. In
contrast—and it is precisely this contrast or shock or emphasis which most sharply indicates how much and what
is at stake in Levinas' "philosophy"—alterity must be ac-

knowledged in terms of what *surpasses* understanding absolutely, what is *superior* to the horizons of being and the truth of being, what exceeds or precedes the beginning of philosophy: the *surplus* or *excellence* of ethical command and the infinite responsibilities it calls forth. The alterity of the Other is not simply recalcitrant to knowledge and caresses; it is a positive force; but its positivity is a moral rather than an ontological or epistemological force. Because philosophy is rooted in the firstness of first philosophy, in the quest for origins, Levinas' claims shift back and forth from negative to positive, from the inadequacy of philosophy to the excellence of ethics. This is the opposition or disturbance which Jacques Derrida, recalling the words of James Joyce, calls "Jewgreek." The subject is traumatized, loses its balance, its moderation, its recuperative powers, its autonomy, its principle and principles, is shaken out of its contemporaneousness with the world and others, owing to the impact of a moral force: the assymetrical "height and destitution" of the Other.

Death, which Levinas had already grasped in terms of the alterity of the other person, becomes murder. "Murder," Levinas writes, in *Totality and Infinity*, "at the origin of death, reveals a cruel world, but one to the scale of human relations. The will. . . exposed to death but not *immediately*, has time to be *for the Other*, and thus to recover meaning despite death. This existence for the Other, this Desire of the other, this goodness liberated from the egoist gravitation, . . . retains a personal character. . . . The Desire into which the threatened will dissolves no longer defends the powers of a will, but, as the goodness whose meaning death cannot efface, has its center outside of itself" (*TI* 236). Thus the egoist will, autonomy, the firstness of first philosophy, always threatened by death, but mortal by nature, does not gather itself into a greater strength, (no strength, in any event, *can* ultimately resist death), but recognizes itself as murderous, recognizes its powers as violent, its autonomy as imperial, and thus becomes good. This transformation or reorientation of the egoist will into good will is not, to be sure, necessary, for necessity is an episte-mological and ontological category. Rather, Levinas will say, shifting from nominative to prescriptive language, the good will is *elected* to its moral status. It is elected at the mo-ment it is capable of seeing the offense of the offended, or the face" (*TI* 247). "Goodness," Levinas writes, "consists in taking up a position in being such that the Other counts more than myself. Goodness thus involves the possibility for the I that is exposed to the alienation of its powers by death to not be for death" (*TI* 247). Thus in death—on Heidegger's home turf, as it were—Levinas discovers the radical and ethical alterity of the Other, rather than the in-dividuation of *Dasein* and openness onto Being, and he dis-covers the radical passivity of the good will.

Exposed to the alterity of the other person, the *I*'s egoist capacities, its powers of synthesis, which have hitherto de-fined the ego for philosophy, are "reconditioned," "put into question," over-exposed, such that the *I* is *first* for-the-other *before* the very firstness of its being for-itself. It is in this ethical reversal, in this "first" which ontologically and epistemologically comes second, or afterwards, in this pe-culiar structure of over-exposure, excessive vulnerability, the anteriority of what comes later, in this first for-the-other before being for-itself, against a for-itself which naturally comes first and whose very telos *is* to come first, that Levinas discovers the irreducible alterity of time. Thus time involves an extraordinary past in a *superlative passivity* which is more passive than, or prior to, the subject's predi-cative and prepredicative syntheses, which seem to come first and which are even defined as the power of coming first, and serve, in one way or another, as the ground of first philosophy.

The *I* commanded by the Other finds itself commanded before itself, despite-itself, before its own self-control, before the very abilities which seem to be its definition and definitiveness. The *I* elected to its responsibilities is elected subject to the Other. It is forced into itself, morally singularized, made responsible, not by itself but despite-itself, an-archically, by the Other.

Thus a radical *passivity*, a radical exposure, prior to all the syntheses which have hitherto defined time, subjectivity, being, and truth for philosophy, and a radical *alterity*, again beyond all the syntheses which have hitherto defined time, subjectivity, being, and truth for philosophy, are related by means of ethics, and thus by means of a time liberated from the present and self-presence, liberated from synthesis and sameness. The irreducible *alterity* of the Other, the time of the Other, impinges on the subject's temporal syntheses from the outside, disrupting its unity with another time, the time of the Other or ethics, the command which comes from on high. And in the same extraordinary moment, the Other's commmand calls forth a subjectivity for-the-other, that is to say, a subjectivity which "fears murder more than death," which recognizes itself as murderous and the Other as vulnerable or destitute, the object of the subject's actual or potential violence, the object of irresponsibility and injustice. Such a reconditioning transformation is not properly ontological or epistemological, rather it is an ethical deformation of being and knowledge, the very "deformalization" of time.

In *Totality and Infinity* it is argued that the rupture of the egoist *I*, its reconditioning in the face of the Other, the reorientation despite-itself of the for-itself to the for-the-other, is effected by means of a positivity, the surplus of ethics, rather than by a negativity or lack which the subject would then recuperate or attempt to recuperate. Levinas focuses more closely on the time structure of this ethical orientation—non-in-difference—in an article which appeared shortly after the publication of *Totality and Infinity*, entitled "The Trace of the Other" (1963). The theses of *To-

tality and Infinity are first repeated in abbreviated form: "To discover such an orientation in the *I* is to identify the *I* with morality. The I before the Other is infinitely responsible."; "The unicity of the I is the fact that no one can answer for me." How, then, does Levinas see a past and a future in this disruption and election of the ego?

How is the structure of ethics the structure of time? The future is the future of he who is always yet to come, he who will never and can never fully present himself, because the subject's ego cannot reach in or reach out to be or anticipate the Other's ego. This inability, however, is not merely an epistemological or ontological failure, a problem of knowledge or a limitation of being. Indeed it is not a failure. The oncoming character of the Other, the Other *qua* future, what Levinas names "illeity," is not merely unforeseeable, which it would be from the point of view of the knowing or grasping ego, it is not merely a question of craft and ruse, the tactics of war, rather the Other is *better* than the ego, and thus exerts moral demands on the ego. The *I* is responsible not only to know the Other, or to share an understanding of the world which the Other also shares, but is responsible to respond to the very alterity of the Other, to an alterity which is always on the verge of presence but never comes to presence, is never reducible to the phenomenality of the face. The face is not, properly, a phenomenon, a noema of the subject's noeses, but a plasticity or enigma which pierces phenomenality with command, from a future which is never present though infinitely close to the present. This oncoming character of the Other—the future—is also what Levinas calls "expression," a meaning-giving which overdetermines any meaning-given. At the same moment, furthermore, the Other forces upon the egoist subject a *past* that was never within the subject's powers of presencing or making present. That is to say, in the face of the Other, goodness emerges as the responsibility of the subject which has *always already* been responsible, prior to any explicit agreements, prior even to the subject's ability to welcome the Other. "The beyond from which a face comes signifies as a trace." Levinas writes in "The Trace of the Other," "A face is in the trace of the utterly bygone, utterly past Absent . . . which cannot be discovered in the self by any introspection." Precisely the obligation the Other inserts into the ego, the obligation which is the very election of the ego, its responsibility to respond to the Other, is suffered by the ego as always already having passed into the ego, as having *already* put the ego into question, an-archically—to the extent that the ego is put into question, that is to say, to the extent that the ego is good. "No memory could follow the trace of this past. It is an immemorial past."

Language

The ethically elected ego is both already obligated and never sufficiently obligated, and such is the very structure of time. A past already in force, a moral force, putting the ego into question, despite-itself, against its synthesizing nature, more passive than its agency, without ever having been present—obligation to the Other—and a future which never becomes and never can become present—the Other's command: such is the structure of ethics and time, disrupting being and knowledge. But such is also the structure, as Levinas' use of the terms "trace" and "expression" indicates, of language, of the significance of signification.

Already in "The Trace of the Other" Levinas characterizes this paradoxical relationship, a relationship with what remains outside of relation while yet being in relation, the non-indifference of one to the other, proximity, in terms of signification (and—we should notice the oncoming wave—in the concluding pages he characterizes it in terms of God). Over the next several years, in a series of articles which will be collected together to become the core of *Oth-*

erwise than Being or Beyond Essence, he focuses on the ethical alterity of the other person (future) and the ethical exposure of the subject (past), thus on the alterity constitutive of time, in terms of language and signification. It is a matter of elaborating more precisely what is meant by "the *trace* of the Other," by the meaningfulness of the plasticity of the face, by expression and command, and by the responsibility to respond to the Other.

As early as *Totality and Infinity,* Levinas conceived the face as equivalent to expression. "Expression manifests the presence of being," he wrote, "but not by simply drawing aside the veil of the phenomenon. It is of itself presence of a face, and hence appeal and teaching, *entry into relation* with me—the ethical relation. And expression does not manifest the presence of being by referring from the sign to the signified; it presents the signifier. The signifier, he who gives a sign, is not signified" (*TI* 181-81). Thus Levinas distinguishes the relation of sign to signified, which is an epistemological and ontological relation, from the extraordinary relation of both the sign and the signified to the signifier, the Other. In *Otherwise than Being or Beyond Essence,* language and signification are understood in yet a more complex fashion.

Levinas realizes that signification at the phenomenal level is not simply a matter of signs referring to what they signify. Such a straightforward correspondence model is precisely what Derrida criticizes in Husserl, showing that the presence of the signified depends at least as much on the meaningful absence of other signs as on an ostensively direct relation of the sign to the signified in intuition. For signs to be significant, Derrida shows, other signs must be absent. That is to say, language is meaningful not because it touches base here and there in a one to one correspondence with things, but because it is a shifting network of signs, signs which not only refer to one another but defer to one another, playing between themselves in various historically determined configurations, where the presence of one sign is meaningful owing to the absence of other signs. Tr.'s play is equivalent to what Heidegger, in his later work, called the "verbality of the verb." "Language," Levinas writes in *Otherwise than Being or Beyond Essence*, "issued from the verbalness of a verb would then not only consist in making being understood, but also in making its essence vibrate" (*OBBE* 35).

But it is not in Derrida's semiotic play or in the Heideggerian verb, in the vibration of absence and presence, that Levinas finds the alterity constitutive of meaning and time. Such a play, despite its inevitable deferral of meaning, despite its vibrancy and essential undecidability, remains an economy, the economy of what is *Said*. But what is Said depends, in its turn, on another sort of absence, the irreducible absence of what in *Totality and Infinity* Levinas called the signifier, that is to say, he who speaks and at the same time commands ethically, putting the ego into question. "It belongs to the very essence of language," Levinas wrote in *Totality and Infinity*, foreshadowing the analyses of *Otherwise than Being or Beyond Essence*, "which consists in continually undoing its phrase by the foreword or the exegesis, in unsaying the said, in attempting to restate without ceremonies what has already been ill understood in the inevitable ceremonial in which the said delights" (*TI* 30). This movement of language is what Levinas now calls *Saying*, the ethical condition of what is Said. "It is the impossibility of the dispersion of time to assemble itself in the present, the insurmountable diachrony of time" (*OBBE* 38).

It is because language depends first on one-being-for-the-other, Saying, the exceptional command of the Other demanding and evoking the subject's irrecuperable responsibility to respond, that there is meaning, the Said, and time, the future and past. The Said, like representation, tends toward the present, toward simultaneity, contemporaneousness, the economy of self-presence, even if it always "fails" in its aims, as Derrida points out, even if it endlessly vibrates, is subject to endless reconfigurations and manifests an irreducible equivocation in being. This deformation in language is not the deformalization to which Levinas points. Saying is never present in the Said, for the Said is too late and too early, is already caught—no matter how subtle or brilliant its vibrancy—within the economy of truth and self-presence. Saying enters the Said otherwise than the vibration or play of the Said: it is traced in the Said, as a subversion, both as the possibility of un-saying or resaying the Said—the pure future—and as the disruption, the *hurt*, to which the egoist subject passively submits, in patience, in suffering, already striking the ego-ist subject in a vulnerability it can never ground or recuperate—the immemorial past. The structure of such a relation—both ethical and significant: the proximity of the Other, non-in-difference, the for-the-other, the Saying of the Said—is what Levinas calls *dia-chrony* or *emphasis*.

In his 1982 paper, "Diachrony and Representation," Levinas focuses on this structure—which produces ethics and language—specifically in terms of the diachrony of time. He begins, as might be expected, with a condensed and schematic recapitulation of his entire itinerary, in order to articulate—in contrast to the time of re-presentation and presencing—the paradoxical alterity of dia-chrony, the pro-totype of all time. For time to be thought as the break up of reality into the irreducible dimensions of past, present, and future, it must finally be thought in terms of a *past which was never present* and a *future which never will be present*. Such, as has by now become clear, is the Other's future and past for the subject despite-itself, the Other's Saying, the Other's command, but only for the good ego, the ego *first* for-the-other, for-the-other-before-itself, the subject subject to the Other, elected to itself. Levinas employs the term "dia-chrony" in opposition to the term "synchrony," just as earlier he posed "mystery" against "possibility," "infinity"

against "totality," "otherwise than being" against "being,"
"Saying" against "Said," and the "Other" against the
"Same." The terms are not on the same plane. The dia-
chrony of time can never be grasped but is only, or *at best*,
undergone in the first person singular.

God

The last stage of Levinas' thought, the alterity of the "to-
God" (à Dieu), extends the significance of the Other's otherness to its furthest reaches. Already in *Totality and Infinity*
Levinas characterized the intersubjective relation as *religion*, the insatiable desire for the absolutely desirable, in
contrast to the satisfactions of ontology, epistemology, and
theology. The central term of that text, "infinity," is explicitly borrowed from Descartes' *Meditations*, where it referred
to the divine—which "dazzled" the Cartesian ego. Levinas
has always been concerned and outspoken about Judaism,
the religion of his birth; *Totality and Infinity*, however, marks
the beginning of what comes to be a more and more explicit
and extensive insertion of God into his properly philosophical writings. But Levinas' God does not appear as a tidal
wave to obliterate the work of all the earlier waves.

As indicated by his attachment to the religious writings
of Franz Rosenzweig, especially *The Star of Redemption*
(1921), and his attachment to the Lithuanian rabbinic tradition, particularly as found in the celebrated work of Rabbi
Hayyim of Volozhyn (1749-1821), the *Nefesh Hahayyim* (published posthumously in 1824) [*The Soul of Life*], God for
Levinas is neither an absolute power nor the object of mystical or dogmatic belief. God, too, is encountered in the alterity of the other person. God Himself "comes to the idea"
in proximity, in the non-in-difference of one to another.
The wholly other, God, shines in the face of the Other.
"The subjection that precedes deliberation about an imperative, measures, so to speak, or attests to, an infinite au-

thority" (*TO* 117), he writes in the section entitled "To-God," in "Diachrony and Representation." The appearance of God, then, is not the appearance of a set of absolute rules or a privileged text, nor is it a revelation which opens the skies, it is, rather, the very excellence of ethics, command without commandments, the love for the Other prior to the love for oneself, "love," as Levinas describes it, recalling Pascal, "without concupiscence." "The futuration of the future," he writes, "is not a 'proof of God's existence,' but 'the fall of God into meaning'" (*TO* 115). Thus to care for one's neighbor more than oneself, to take on responsibility for the Other, ethics, and to take on the Other's responsibilities, justice, is to enter into a *sacred* rather than an ontological or epistemological history. "The existence of God," Levinas has said in a recent interview, "is sacred history itself, the sacrednesss of man's relation to man through which God may pass."

Sacred history, the ethical time and significance of sociality, for Levinas, is not the voyage of an Odysseus, who ventures out courageously but only in order to finally return home, where he began his voyage; but the journey of an Abram, who leaves his ancestral home for good, who never returns and never arrives at his destination, who encounters and is subject to the absolute alterity of God, who overthrows the idols and is transformed to becomes his better self, Abraham. Thus Levinas' works become "consecrated," as he says of Rabbi Hayyim's great work, "to a God who claims to be dependent on humans, on the persons who, since they are infinitely responsible, support the universe."

Thinking time in relation to the other person, thinking time and the obligations of social life together, means exceeding all the categories and structures which have thus far determined thought itself. It means exceeding the *neces-*

sity of thought's necessary categories and structures, for the sake of a greater necessity, and exceeding the *priority* of thought's a priori conditions and transcendentality, for the sake of a greater priority. Not, certainly, to enter a wild no man's land where anything and everything is permitted, where thought becomes radically otherwise than thinking, a vertiginous leap toward "action," "dance," or "violence," where the rupture of thought makes all names possible by making them all equally unintelligible; but, as Levinas would have it, to be awakened to an even more vigilant thinking, to a more attentive, alert, sensitive awareness, to a thinking stripped of its formality and ceremonies, stripped to the rawest nerve, to an unsupportable suffering and vulnerability, a thinking which *thinks otherwise* than thought itself, because suffering the inversion and election of being for-the-other before itself.

To think otherwise, for Levinas, is to undergo the *emphasis*, the *hyperbole*, the *superlative*, the *excellence* which escapes thought while determining it. It is to recognize the dative, the "to the other" and the "for the other," which overdetermines the nominative. It is to enter into a *disorientation* which is neither an opinion, a prejudice, a dogma, nor a truth, but the wonder proper to ethical significance.

This perpetual dis-orientation is responsibility. But the responsibility Levinas has in mind is paradoxically a *greater* responsibility than the already infinite responsibilities set by *ratio* in its quest for the truth of being, in its call for sufficient reasons and historical authenticity. The responsibility Levinas discerns in thinking, then, is not just another *more rigorous* attention to method and evidence, another epistemological duty added to the responsibilities which guide and give the reasons for reason, the autonomy of the measured life. Rather, there is an *other* responsibility, an unmeasured and unmeasurable responsibility, one directed from and toward the *outside* of thought, from and toward the irreducible alterity of the other person. There are obligations greater than the infinite responsibility to think and be on one's own, greater, then, than all the traditional philosophic responsibilities, greater because *better.* The alterity which is time itself, breaks up reality into an irrecuperable past and an unreachable future, disrupts the natural complacency of being, overloads it, charging it with a greater responsibility than its capacities can handle. This will mean that less than a hundred years after its liberation from twenty five centuries of servitude to the categories of knowledge, from *eternity* and *essential being,* time must be rethought beyond its recent tutelage to the structures of existential understanding, from *history* and *temporality.* Time must be liberated from its liberators, for time is not a matter of freedom.

Levinas demands further thought, demands that thought go further—than it has ever gone or *can* go. Yet his thought is not another nuance in hyperconsciousness; disorientation and disorder are familiar in our day. Ours is an age of dis-aster—an age without a guiding star, an age whose firmament has been shaken and is shaking, an unmoored epoch, so seemingly without bearings, where the future of humanity, if not life itself, is in question. We live, Levinas has written in a recent article, in "the century which in thirty years has known two world wars, the totalitarianisms of right and left, Hitlerism and Stalinism, Hiroshima, the Goulag, the genocides of Auschwitz and Cambodia." It has never been more difficult to think—but not just because the quantity of accumulated and available information has increased geometrically and geographically, as it has; nor only because, having tried and exhausted more than two millenia of self-interpretations, and having recently tried several brilliant and varied renewals, thought no longer knows what to think of itself, no longer has words for itself, can push its hyper-self-reflection no further; but, more profoundly, because thought can no longer think *in good conscience.* Good conscience is not good enough.

To live the *end* of metaphysics, its fulfilment and termination, requires, Levinas insists, that we take *bad conscience* seriously, that we recognize the full extent and weight of our debts and obligations to the Other and to Others, that we value goodness and justice above being and order.

Preface (1979)

To write a preface on the occasion of the republication of something one published thirty years earlier is almost to write the preface to someone else's book. Except that one sees its shortcomings more quickly and feels them more painfully.

The text you are about to read reproduces the steno-graphic record of four lectures given under the title "Time and the Other" in 1946/47, during the first year of the Philosophical College founded by Jean Wahl in the Latin Quarter, Paris. It appeared in 1948 in a collection entitled *Le Choix, le Monde, l'Existence*,[1] the first of the Philosophical College publications. I was happy to have this article accompany those of Jeanne Hersch, Alphonse de Waelhens, and Jean Wahl himself.[2] The style (or nonstyle) of this writ-

---

[1] Cahiers du Collège Philosophique (Grenoble-Paris: Arthaud, 1947), pp. 125–96.

[2] Jeanne Hersch (1910–) has taught at a number of universities in Europe and the United States; she is currently active in UNESCO. She has translated Karl Jaspers into French, and is the author of *L'illusion philosophique* (1936), *L'être et la forme* (1946), and *La foi a l'épreuve du XX' siécle* (1983), among other works.

Alphonse de Waelhens (1911–) professor of philosophy at the University of Saint-Louis in Brussels, has written several studies in contemporary philosophy, most notably books on Martin Heidegger (*La philosophie de Martin Heidegger*, 1942) and Maurice Merleau-Ponty (*Une philosophie de la'ambiguité*, 1951).

ing will surely be, for many, abrupt or maladroit in certain turns of phrase. In these essays there are also theses whose contexts have neither been formulated, nor their openings explored to the end, nor have they a systematic dissemination. Take these remarks as a preliminary note signaling all the flaws that since 1948 the aging of the text has probably accentuated.

If I nonetheless approved the idea of its republication, and in book form, and have foregone rejuvenating it, this because I still adhere to the main project of which it is—in the midst of diverse movements of thought—the birth and first formulation, and because its exposition progressively improves as one advances through its pages written in haste. Is time the very limitation of finite being or is it the relationship of finite being to God? It is a relationship that, nevertheless, would not secure for a being an infinitude as opposed to finitude, an auto-sufficiency as opposed to need, but that would signify, beyond satisfaction and dissatisfaction, the surplus of sociality. This way of examining time still seems to me today to be the vital problem. *Time and the Other* presents time not as the ontological horizon of the *being of a being* [l' *"être de l'étant"*] but as a mode of the *beyond being* [l' *"au delà de l'être"*], as the relationship of "thought" to the other [*Autre*],[3] and—through the diverse

[3] I have always translated *autrui* as the "Other," with an uppercase "O," and *autre* as "other," with a lowercase "o" (except for the title of this book and one section heading in part 3. Whenever "other" [*Autre*] is capitalized in French, I have supplied the term in brackets. *Autrui* refers to the personal other, the other person; *autre* refers to otherness in general, to alterity.

Jean Wahl (1888–1974), a poet, existential philosopher, expositor of existential philosophies, and historian of philosophy, was professor of philosophy at the Sorbonne from 1936 until his death. Levinas always speaks of Wahl with much personal admiration. *Totality and Infinity* is dedicated to Marcelle and Jean Wahl. See also Levinas, "Jean Wahl et le sentiment," *Cahiers du Sud*, vol. 42, no. 331 (1955) 453–59, reprinted in *Noms propres*

figures of the sociality facing the face of the other person: eroticism, paternity, responsibility for the neighbor—as the relationship to the Wholely other *[Tout Autre]*, the Transcendent, the Infinite. It is a relation or religion that is not structured like knowing—that is, an intentionality. Knowing conceals re-presentation and reduces the *other* to presence and co-presence. Time, on the contrary, in its dia-chrony, would signify a relationship that does not compromise the other's alterity, while still assuring its nonindifference to "thought."

As a modality of finite being, time would indeed signify the dispersion of *the being of a being* into mutually exclusive moments, which are, besides, as instants unstable and unfaithful even to themselves, each expelled into the past out of their own presence, yet furnishing the fulgurating idea— and the non-sense and sense, the death and life—of this presence that they would thus suggest. But then eternity— the idea of which, without borrowing anything from lived duration *[la durée vécue]*, the intellect would claim to possess a priori: the idea of a *mode of being*, where the multiple is one and which would confer on the present its full sense —is it not always suspect of only dissimulating the fulguration of the instant, its half-truth, which is retained in an imagination capable of playing in the intemporal and of deluding itself about a gathering of the nongatherable? In the final account, would not this eternity and this intellectual God, composed of these abstract and inconstant half-instants of the temporal dispersion, be an abstract eternity and a dead God?

The main thesis caught sight of in *Time and the Other*, on

(Montpellier: Fata Morgana, 1976), pp. 165-74; and the paper Levinas gave after Wahl's death, "Jean Wahl: Sans avoir ni être," in *Jean Wahl et Gabriel Marcel*, edited by Jeanne Hersch (Paris: Editions Beauchesne, 1976), pp. 13-31. Also see footnote 7, below.

the contrary, consists in thinking time not as a degradation of eternity, but as the relationship to *that* which—of itself unassimilable, absolutely other—would not allow itself to be assimilated by experience; or to *that* which—of itself infinite—would not allow itself to be com-prehended. That is, however, if this Infinite or this other *[Autre]* must still tolerate what we designate by using the demonstrative "*that*," like a simple object, or what we hitch to it with a definite or indefinite article to give it body. It is a relationship with the In-visible, where invisibility results not from some incapacity of human knowledge, but from the inaptitude of knowledge as such— from its in-adequation—to the Infinity of the absolutely other, and from the absurdity that an event such as coincidence would have here. This impossibility of coinciding and this inadequation are not simply negative notions, but have a meaning in the *phenomenon* of noncoincidence *given* in the dia-chrony of time. Time signifies this *always* of noncoincidence, but also the *always* of the *relationship*, an aspiration and an awaiting, a thread finer than an ideal line that diachrony does not cut. Diachrony preserves this thread in the paradox of a relationship that is different from all the other relationships of our logic and psychology, which, by way of an ultimate community, at the very least confer synchrony on their terms. Here there is a relationship without terms, an awaiting without an awaited, an insatiable aspiration. It is a distance that is also a proximity—which is not a coincidence or a lost union but signifies, as I have said, all the surplus or all the *goodness* of an original proximity. Is not the difficulty and height of religion that dia-chrony is *more* than a synchronism, that proximity is *more precious* than the fact of being given, that allegiance to the unequalled is *better* than   a self-consciousness? All descriptions of this "distance-proximity" could not be elsewise than approximate or metaphorical, since the dia-chrony of time in them is the non-figural meaning, the literal meaning, the model.[4]

The "movement" of time understood as transcendence toward the Infinity of the "wholly other" [tout Autre] does not temporalize in a linear way, does not resemble the straightforwardness of the intentional ray. Its way of signifying, marked by the *mystery* of death, makes a detour by entering into the ethical adventure of the relationship to the other person.[5]

Temporal transcendence is described in my 1948 essay only through insights that remain at best preparatory. They are guided by the analogy between the transcendence that signifies dia-chrony and the distance of the Other's alterity, as well as by the insistences upon the link—incomparable to that which links the terms of every relationship—that traverses the interval of this transcendence.[5]

I did not want to modify the itinerary that follows the expression of these ideas. It seems to me to bear witness to a certain climate of openness that the Montagne Sainte-Geneviève quarter of Paris offered shortly after the Liberation. Jean Wahl's Philosophical College was a reflection of it and one of its centers. One heard the inimitable sonority of

[4]Levinas: Not all the negations occurring in the description of this "relationship with the infinite" are confined to the formal and logical sense of negation, and constitute a negative theology! They say all that a logical language—our language—can express, through a saying and an unsaying, of the dia-chrony that shows itself in the patience of awaiting and is the very length of time, neither reducing to anticipation (already a way of "making present"), nor concealing a *representation* of the awaited or the desired (this representation would be a pure "presentification"). The awaited and desired would already be *terms*; awaiting and aspiration would be a finality, not a relationship to the Infinite.

[5]Levinas: See my *Otherwise than Being or Beyond Essence* (French original, 1974) [translated by A. Lingis (The Hague; Martinus Nijhoff, 1981)] and, more particularly, my study "God and Philosophy," which appeared in 1975 in *Le Nouveau Commerce*, no. 30/31 [translated by R. Cohen and A. Lingis, in *The Collected Philosophical Papers of Emmanuel Levinas*, edited by A. Lingis (The Hague: Martinus Nijhoff, 1986)].

Vladimir Jankelevitch's lofty and inspired speech, uttering
the *unheard* in the Bergsonian message, formulating the in-
effable, and drawing a packed hall at the Philosophical College;" and Jean Wahl hailing the very multiplicity of
tendencies in "living philosophy," stressing the privileged
kinship between philosophy and the diverse forms of art.
He loved following the transitions from one to the other. By
his whole attitude he seemed to invite one to audacious
"*intellectual* experimentation" and risky prospection. Husserlian phenomenology and, thanks to Sartre and
Merleau-Ponty, the philosophy of existence,[7] and even the
first statements of Heidegger's fundamental ontology, then
promised new philosophical possibilities. The words desig-
nating what people were always concerned with, without
daring to imagine it in a speculative discourse, took the
rank of categories. Without circumlocution—and often
without precaution—and although taking some liberties
with the academic rules, but also without submitting to the
tyranny of the then fashionable watchwords, one could
give oneself—and propose to others—ideas "to be exca-
vated," "to be deepened," or "to be explored," as Gabriel
Marcel often designates them in his *Metaphysical Journal*.[8]

It is advisable to read the diverse themes of *Time and the*

"Vladimir Jankelevitch (1903-1986), a musician and philosopher, began
his publishing career with *Henri Bergson* (1931), praised in its Preface by
Henri Bergson himself. Known for his many subtle psychological and
moral studies of such subjects as time and boredom, his main work is
probably *Traité des vertues* (1949).

[7]Given the prominence of existential philosophy at the time, and
Levinas' close personal relationship with Jean Wahl, the reader may take
interest in the latter's small 1947 book, *A Short History of Existentialism*,
translated by F. Williams and S. Maron (New York: Philosophical Library,
1949), in which Levinas appears as a discussant (pp. 47-53); and, among
others, Wahl's *Philosophies of Existence*, translated by F. Lory (New York:
Schocken Books, 1969) (French original, 1954).

[8]Gabriel Marcel, *Metaphysical Journal*, translated by B. Wall (Chicago:
Henry Regnery Company, 1952) [Librairie Gallimard: Paris, 1927]. Levinas
attended the Saturday evening gatherings of the philosophical avant-
garde at Marcel's house in the 1930s.

Other through which my main thesis advances—with detours—in the spirit of those years of openness. There is what is said of subjectivity: the mastery of the Ego over being's anonymous *there is*, forthwith the reversal of the Self over the Ego, the encumbrance of the Ego by the self-same and, thus, a materialist materiality and a solitude of immanence, the irremissible weight of being in work, pain, and suffering. Next there is what is said of the world: the transcendence of nourishments and knowledge, an experience in the heart of enjoyment, a knowing and a return to self, a solitude in the light of knowing absorbing every *other*, the solitude of a reason essentially *one*. Then there is what is said of death: not a pure nothingness but an unassumable mystery and, in this sense, the eventuality of the event at the point of making an irruption within the Sameness of immanence, of interrupting the monotony and the tick-tock of solitary instants—the eventuality of the *wholely other*, of the future, the temporality of time where diachrony precisely describes the relationship with what remains absolutely outside. Finally there is what is said of the relationship with the Other, the feminine, the child, of the fecundity of the Ego, the concrete modality of diachrony, the articulations or inevitable digressions of the transcendence of time; neither an ecstasis, where the Same is absorbed in the other [*Autre*], nor a knowledge, where the other [*Autre*] belongs to the Same—a relationship without relation, an insatiable desire, or the proximity of the Infinite. These are theses that have not all been taken up later in their first form, that since then may have been revealed as inseparable from more complex and older problems, and as demanding a less improvised expression and especially a different thought.

I should like to stress two points, in the last pages of these early lectures, that seem important to me. They concern the way in which the phenomenology of alterity and its transcendence was there attempted.

Human alterity is not thought starting with the purely
formal and logical alterity by which some terms are distin-
guished from others in every multiplicity (where each one
is already other as the bearer of different attributes or, in a
multiplicity of equal terms, where each one is other than
the other through its individuation). The notion of a transcendent alterity—one that opens time—is at first sought
starting with an *alterity-content*—that is, starting with femininity. Femininity—and one would have to see in what
sense this can be said of masculinity or of virility; that is, of
the differences between the sexes in general—appeared to
me as a difference contrasting strongly with other differences, not merely as a quality different from all others, but
as the very quality of difference. This idea should make the
notion of the couple as distinct as possible from every
purely numerical duality. The notion of the sociality of two,
which is probably necessary for the exceptional epiphany
of the face—abstract and chaste nudity—emerges from sexual differences, and is essential to eroticism and to all instances of alterity—again as quality and not as a simply
logical distinction—borne by the "thou shalt not kill" that
the very silence of the face says. Here is a significant ethical
radiance within eroticism and the libido. Through it humanity enters into the society of two and sustains it, autho-
rizes it, perhaps, at least putting into question the
simplicity of contemporary paneroticism.*

I should like finally to stress a structure of transcendence
that in *Time and the Other* has been caught sight of starting
with paternity: the possible offered to the son and placed
beyond what is assumable by the father still remains the *father's* in a certain sense. Precisely in the sense of kinship.
The father's—or non-indifferent—is a possibility that another assumes: through the son there occurs a possibility
beyond the possible! This would be a non-indifference that

*See note 69, below.

does not issue from the social rules governing kinship, but probably founds these rules—a non-indifference through which the "beyond the possible" is possible to the Ego. This is what, starting with the—nonbiological—notion of the Ego's fecundity, puts into question the very idea of *power* [*pouvoir*], such as it is embodied in transcendental subjectivity, the center and source of intentional acts.

Emmanuel Levinas 1979[10]

[10]For other recent general comments by Levinas on *Time and the Other*, see the fourth 1981 radio broadcast interview by Philippe Nemo in Levinas, *Ethics and Infinity*, translated by R. Cohen (Pittsburgh: Duquesne University Press, 1985), pp. 55–62.

[PART I]

The aim of these lectures is to show that time is not
the achievement of an isolated and lone subject, but
that it is the very relationship of the subject with the
Other.[1]

This thesis is in no way sociological. It is not a matter of
saying how time is chopped up and parceled out thanks to
the notions we derive from society, how society allows us to
make a representation of time. It is not a matter of our idea
of time but of time itself.

To uphold this thesis it will be necessary, on the one
hand, to deepen the notion of solitude and, on the other, to
consider the opportunities that time offers to solitude.

The analyses I am about to undertake will not be anthropological but ontological. I do believe in the existence of ontological problems and structures, but not in the sense that
realists—purely and simply describing given being—
ascribe to ontology. It is a matter of affirming that *being* is
not an empty notion, that it has its own dialectic; and that
notions like solitude and collectivity belong to a certain moment of this dialectic and are not merely psychological notions, like the need one can have for the Other or, implied
in this need, like a prescience, presentiment, or anticipation of the other. I want to present solitude as a category of
being, to show its place in a dialectic of being, or rather—
because the word "dialectic" has a more determinate
meaning—to show the place of solitude in the general
economy of being.

[1]See note 2 of the Preface, above.

Thus from the start I repudiate the Heideggerian conception that views solitude in the midst of a prior relationship with the other. Though anthropologically incontestable, the conception seems to me ontologically obscure. The relationship with the Other is indeed posed by Heidegger as an ontological structure of *Dasein*,[2] but practically it plays no role in the drama of being or in the existential analytic. All the analyses of *Being and Time*[3] are worked out either for the sake of the impersonality of everyday life or for the sake of solitary *Dasein*. Then again, does solitude derive its tragic character from nothingness or from the privation of the Other that death accentuates? There is at least an ambiguity. I find here an invitation to go beyond the definition of solitude by sociality and of sociality by solitude. Finally, the other in Heidegger appears in the essential situation of *Miteinandersein*, reciprocally being with one another.... The preposition *mit* (with) here describes the relationship.[4]

[2]Levinas, like almost everyone else who refers to Heidegger in French (or in English for that matter) leaves the term *Dasein* untranslated. I shall do the same. *Dasein* refers to human being, literally meaning "there-being"; it is a term used to highlight the central Heideggerian notion that human existence is always in-the-world and not enclosed within a subject "in here" opposed to objects "out there."

[3]Martin Heidegger, *Being and Time,* translated by J. Maquarrie and E. Robinson (New York: Harper and Row, 1962).
It is perhaps of some interest to note that *Being and Time* had not been translated into French at the time of Levinas' lectures. Indeed, it has taken more than half a century to have *Being and Time* translated into French in its entirety. In 1938 sections 45–53 and 72–77 were translated by H. Corbin and included as part of a volume of Heidegger's writings entitled *Qu'est-ce que la métaphysique?* (Paris: Gallimard). In 1964 sections 1–44 (the "Introduction" and "Division One," the *Dasein* analytic) were translated by A. de Waelhens, and R. Boehm, and published as a volume entitled *L'Etre et le Temps* ["Being and Time"] (Paris: Gallimard). Despite its title, this latter volume is only a truncated version of the original text. The complete text, entitled *Etre et temps*, appeared in 1983 translated and published by E. Martineau, and then three years later in a new translation by F. Vezin (Paris: Gallimard, 1986).

[4]See Heidegger, *Being and Time,* section 26 (pp. 153–63). Levinas will return to Heidegger's notion of *Miteinandersein* at the end of *Time and the Other* (p. 93).

It is thus an association of side by side, around something, around a common term and, more precisely, for Heidegger, around the truth. It is not the face-to-face relationship, where each contributes everything, except the private fact of one's existence. I hope to show, for my part, that it is not the preposition *mit* that should describe the original relationship with the other.

My way of proceeding will lead me to developments that will perhaps be fairly arduous. They will not have the brilliant pathos of anthropological developments. But in return I should be able to say something else about solitude than its unhappiness and opposition to collectivity, to that collectivity whose happiness one usually says is in opposition to solitude.

In thus going back to the ontological root of solitude I hope to glimpse wherein this solitude can be exceeded. Let me say at once what this exceeding will not be. It will not be a knowledge, because through knowledge, whether one wants it or not, the object is absorbed by the subject and duality disappears. It will not be an ecstasis, because in ecstasis the subject is absorbed in the object and recovers itself in its unity. All these relationships result in the disappearance of the other.

This is when I come up against the problems of suffering and death. Not because these are very lofty themes, permitting brilliant and fashionable expositions, but because in the phenomenon of death solitude finds itself bordering on the edge of a mystery. This mystery is not properly understood negatively, as what is unknown. I shall have to establish its positive significance. This notion will allow me to catch sight of a relationship in the subject that will not be reduced to a pure and simple return to solitude. Before the death that will be mystery and not necessarily nothingness, the absorption of one term by the other does not come about. I shall show finally how the duality evinced in death becomes the relationship with the other and time.

The dialectic these developments may contain is in any case not Hegelian. It is not a matter of traversing a series of contradictions, or of reconciling them while stopping History. On the contrary, it is toward a pluralism that does not merge into unity that I should like to make my way and, if this can be dared, break with Parmenides.

THE SOLITUDE OF EXISTING

In what does the acuity of solitude consist? It is banal to say we never exist in the singular. We are surrounded by beings and things with which we maintain relationships. Through sight, touch, sympathy and cooperative work, we are with others. All these relationships are transitive: I touch an object, I see the other. But I *am* not the other. I am all alone. It is thus the being in me, the fact that I exist, my *existing*, that constitutes the absolutely intransitive element, something without intentionality or relationship. One can exchange everything between beings except existing. In this sense, to be is to be isolated by existing. Inasmuch as I am, I am a monad. It is by existing that I am without windows and doors, and not by some content in me that would be incommunicable. If it is incommunicable, it is because it is rooted in my being, which is what is most private in me. In this way every enlargement of my knowledge or of my means of self-expression remains without effect on my relationship with existing, the interior relationship par excellence.

Primitive mentality—or at least the interpretation Levy-Bruhl gave of it[5]—seemed to shake the foundation of our

[5]See Lucien Levy-Bruhl, *How Natives Think*, translated by L. A. Clare, introduction by C. Scott Littleton (Princeton University Press, 1985); originally published in 1910 as *Les fonctions mentales dans les sociétes inférieures*; English translation originally published in 1925. Levinas again refers to Levy-Bruhl's notion of a prelogical participatory existence, where the principle of noncontradiction is inoperative, in *Existence and Existents*, p. 60, and in *Totality and Infinity*, p. 276. See also Levinas, "Levy-Bruhl et la phi-

concepts because it appeared to contribute the idea of a transitive existence. One had the impression that through participation the subject not only sees the other, but *is* the other. This notion is more important to primitive mentality than is the notion of the prelogical or the mystical. Nonetheless it does not deliver us from solitude. A modern consciousness, at least, could not abdicate its secrecy and solitude at so little cost. And to the extent that the experience of participation may be real today, it coincides with ecstatic fusion. It does not sufficiently maintain the duality of terms. If we leave monadology we arrive at monism.

Existing resists every relationship and multiplicity. It concerns no one other than the existent. Solitude therefore appears neither as the factual isolation of a Robinson Crusoe nor as the incommunicability of a content of consciousness, but as the indissoluble unity between the existent and its work of existing. To take up the existing in the existent is to enclose it within unity and to let Parmenides escape every parricide his descendants would be tempted to commit against him. Solitude lies in the very fact that there are existents. To conceive a situation wherein solitude is overcome is to test the very principle of the tie between the existent and its existing. It is to move toward an ontological event wherein the existent contracts existence. The event by which the existent contracts its existing I call *hypostasis*.[6]

---

[6]Given that this term is little used in philosophy today and, given Levinas' distinctive use of it to refer to the origin of an entity that is neither substantial nor insubstantial, the following information, taken from an article entitled "Substance and Attribute," by D.J. O'Connor (*The Encyclopedia of Philosophy*, vol. 8, edited by P. Edwards [New York: Macmillan Publishing Co., 1972], p. 36) may prove helpful: "It is interesting to note that the principal term for substance in the writings of Aristotle is *ousia*, a word which in earlier Greek writers means 'property' in the legal sense of the word, that which is owned.... The Latin word *substantia*, from which the English term is derived, is a literal translation of the Greek word *hypos-*

Perception and science always start with existents already
supplied with their private existence. Is this tie between
what exists and its existing indissoluble? Can one go back
to hypostasis?

EXISTING WITHOUT EXISTENTS

We return again to Heidegger. One cannot ignore his
distinction—which I have already used—between *Sein* and
Seindes, Being and being, but which for reasons of euphony
I prefer to render as *existing* and *existent*, without ascribing
a specifically existentialist meaning to these terms.[7]
Heidegger distinguishes subjects and objects—the beings
that are, existents—from their very work of being. The first
are expressed by substantives or substantivated participles,
the other by a verb. This distinction, which is posited from
the start of *Being and Time*,[8] permits dispelling certain of the
equivocations of philosophy in the course of its history,
where one started with existing to arrive at the existent possessing existing fully, God.

   The most profound thing about *Being and Time* for me is

tasis ("standing under"). This term acquired its philosophical connota-
tions in later Greek and occurs principally in controversies among early
Christian theologians about the real nature of Christ." The later Greek
who gave the term *hypostasis* its philosophical connotation was Plotinus.
Though Levinas rarely mentions Plotinus, it would be interesting to compare their accounts of the emergence of distinct entities. It would also be
interesting to compare the commitments involved in Heidegger's charac-
terization of *Dasein*'s being in terms of authenticity *(Eigentlichkeit)*, own-
ness or property, as well as his use of the term *ousia*, with Levinas'
commitment to the term *hypostasis* to understand the individuation of existence.

   [7]For comments on this particular sentence, and an important analysis
and "semiotic critique" of much else in Levinas, see Jacques Derrida's 1964
essay, "Violence and Metaphysics: An Essay on the Thought of Emmanuel Levinas," republished in his *Writing and Difference*, translated by A.
Bass (University of Chicago Press, 1978) pp. 79–153.

   [8]See Heidegger, *Being and Time*, translator's note 1 on pp. 19 and 22.

this Heideggerian distinction. But in Heidegger there is a distinction, not a separation.[9] Existing is always grasped in the existent, and for the existent that is a human being the Heideggerian term *Jemeinigkeit*[10] precisely expresses the fact that existing is always possessed by someone. I do not think Heidegger can admit an existing without existents, which to him would seem absurd. However, there is a notion—*Geworfenheit*[11]—"expression of a certain Heidegger," according to Jankelevitch—that is usually translated "dereliction" or "desertion." One then stresses a consequence of *Geworfenheit*. One must understand *Geworfenheit* as the "fact-of-being-thrown-in". . . existence.[12] It is as if the existent appeared only in an existence that precedes it, as though existence were independent of the existent, and the existent that finds itself thrown there could never become master of existence. It is precisely because of this that there is desertion and abandonment. Thus dawns the idea of an existing that occurs without us, without a subject, an exist-

[9]The notion of *separation* is of the utmost epistemological and ontological importance in Levinas' philosophy.

The idea is doubtlessly borrowed from Franz Rosenzweig, whose *The Star of Redemption*, published in 1921, exerted an enormous influence on Levinas. Rosenzweig aimed to think humankind, the world, and God, each in their own terms—that is, in their radical separation from one another; as well as in their interrelations.

Levinas likewise here attempts to think existence independent of existents—that is, in its separation from the world and others (and God to the extent that God is an existent). Later in this text—and elsewhere in other texts—he attempts to think the human being, qua "hypostasis," in independence, in separation from the world and others (and God).

This structure of separation puts Levinas in a difficult position relative to philosophy and its history, which has perhaps defined itself from its inception as intellectual vision of the one, the whole, the comprehensive. Levinas attempts to both reject Parmenides (the One) and remain a philosopher. Whether and how this is possible is the central issue of the collection of secondary articles on Levinas, *Face to Face with Levinas*, edited by R. Cohen (Albany; State University of New York Press, 1986).

[10]"Mineness, see Heidegger, *Being and Time*, pp. 68 and 284.

[11]Heidegger, *Being and Time*, pp. 174, 223, 330–33.

[12]The English translators of *Being and Time* have indeed used the term "throwness" to translate *Geworfenheit*.

ing without existents. Without doubt Jean Wahl would say that an existing without existents is only a word. The term "word" is surely upsetting because it is pejorative. But on the whole I am in agreement with Wahl. Only one should first determine the place of the word in the general economy of being.[13] I would also gladly say that existing does not exist. It is the existent that exists. And the fact of having recourse to what does not exist, in order to understand what does exist, hardly constitutes a revolution in philosophy. Idealist philosophy on the whole has been a way of grounding being on something that does not have being.

How are we going to approach this existing without existents? Let us imagine all things, beings and persons, returning to nothingness.[14] What remains after this imaginary destruction of everything is not something, but the fact that there is [il y a].[15] The absence of everything returns as a presence, as the place where the bottom has dropped out of everything, an atmospheric density, a plenitude of the void, or the murmur of silence. There is, after this destruction of things and beings, the impersonal "field of forces"[16] of existing. There is something that is neither sub-

[13] Of course, philosophy has already said a great deal about the role of the word and its relationship to being. Franz Rosenzweig's thoughts on words, however, may not be especially well known to philosophers. See The Star of Redemption, translated by W.W. Halo (Boston: Beacon Press, 1972; Notre Dame: Notre Dame Press, 1985), especially book 2 of part 2 (pp. 156–204); and Understanding the Sick and the Healthy, edited by N.N. Glatzer (New York: Noonday Press, 1954), especially chapters 3 (pp. 35–41) and 6 (pp. 53–62).

[14] This technique of approaching existence without existents by means of the imagination is also employed in Existence and Existents, pp. 57–58.

[15] In 1946 Levinas published an article entitled "Il y a" (Deucalion, vol. 1, pp. 141–54), which he later incorporated into Existence and Existents (pp. 17–18, 57–64). The there is again appears in Totality and Infinity, where it is also called "the elemental." It is a notion of continued significance for all Levinas' subsequent thought, and is always assumed when it is not explicitly invoked.

[16] This expression is doubtlessly meant to recall, at least, Kant's account of the transcendental esthetic, at the beginning of The Critique of Pure Reason; Hegel's account of "Force and The Understanding," at the beginning

ject nor substantive. The fact of existing imposes itself when there is no longer anything. And it is anonymous: there is neither anyone nor anything that takes this existence upon itself. It is impersonal like "it is raining" or "it is hot."[17] Existing returns no matter with what negation one dismisses it. There is, as the irremissibility of pure existing.[18]

In evoking the anonymity of this existing, I am not at all thinking of the indeterminate ground spoken of in philosophy textbooks, where perception carves out things. This indeterminate ground is already a being [un être]—an entity [un étant]—a something. It already falls under the category

[17]Compare this with Friedrich Nietzsche, *The Will to Power* (Kaufmann and Hollingdale translation), section 635; or *Beyond Good and Evil*, sections 16 and 17.

Nietzsche too (and Freud and Marx, in their way) was struck by the impersonality of being. The "I" for Nietzsche is always the product of a preconscious "it" made up of forces in contention. Gilles Deleuze makes much of this in his *Nietzsche and Philosophy*, translated by H. Tomlinson (New York: Columbia University Press, 1983). Also in this regard, see A. Lingis, "The Will to Power" in *The New Nietzsche*, edited by D.B. Allison (Cambridge: The MIT Press, 1985), pp. 37–63.

Levinas has always kept a critical distance from Nietzsche, especially seeing in his thought an attempt to undermine the universal intention of truth. See Levinas, "Quelques réflexions sur la philosphie de l'hitlérisme" ["Some Reflections on the Philosophy of Hitlerism"] in *Esprit*, vol. 2, no. 26 (November 1934), pp. 199–208; see also the comments on Levinas' article by Georges Batailles, "Nietzsche et les fascistes" ["Nietzsche and the Fascists"] in *Acephale*, vol. 2 (January 1937) pp. 3–13; English translation in Batailles, *Visions of Excess: Selected Writings, 1927–1939*, edited and translated by A. Stoekl (Minneapolis: University of Minnesota Press, 1985), pp. 182–96, especially the last 3 pages.

[18]These descriptions of the "there is" provide a *phenomenological* counterpart to Henri Bergson's 1907 arguments against, and his psychologistic account of, the idea of "nothing" in *Creative Evolution* (translated by A. Mitchell [New York: Random House, 1944] pp. 296–324). Levinas several times acknowledges Bergson's importance for him.

Though Levinas radically rejects Parmenides' philosophically decisive concept of the One, we can see in the notion of the "there is" an acceptance of Parmenides' sanction against the path of nonbeing.

of *The Phenomenology of Spirit* (especially sections 136–41); and Nietzsche's account of will to power (see the following note).

of the substantive. It already has that elementary personality characteristic of every existent. The existing that I am trying to approach is the very work of being, which cannot be expressed by a substantive but is verbal. This existing cannot be purely and simply affirmed, because one always affirms a *being* [*étant*]. But it imposes itself because one cannot deny it. Behind every negation this ambience of being, this being as a "field of forces," reappears, as the field of every affirmation and negation. It is never attached to an *object that is*, and because of this I call it anonymous.

Let us approach this situation from another slant. Let us take insomnia.[19] This time it is not a matter of an imagined experience. Insomnia is constituted by the consciousness that it will never finish—that is, that there is no longer any way of withdrawing from the vigilance to which one is held. Vigilance without end. From the moment one is riveted there, one loses all notion of a starting or finishing point. The present is welded to the past, is entirely the heritage of that past: it renews nothing. It is always the same present or the same past that endures. A memory would already be a liberation with regard to the past. Here, time begins nowhere, nothing moves away or shades off. Only the exterior noises that may mark insomnia introduce beginnings in this situation without beginnings or end, in this immortality from which one cannot escape,[20] very similar to the *there is*, the impersonal existence about which I was just speaking.

I am going to characterize the *there is*, and the way that existing is affirmed in its own annihilation, by a vigilance

[19]In *Existence and Existents*, too, Levinas turns to an account of "the night" (pp. 58–61) after invoking the imaginative "experience" of nothingness.

[20]In *Existence and Existents* Levinas develops this striking but nascent thought into a third and final access to the "there is": the "impossibility of death" (pp. 61–62).

without possible recourse to sleep. That is to say, by a vigilance without refuge in unconsciousness, without the possibility of withdrawing into sleep as into a private domain. This existing is not an *in-itself* [*en-soi*], which is already peace; it is precisely the absence of all self, a *without-self* [*sans-soi*]. One can also characterize existing by the notion of eternity, since existing without existents is without a starting point. An eternal subject is a *contradictio in adjecto*, for a subject is already a beginning. The eternal subject not only cannot begin anything outside itself, it is impossible in itself, for as a subject it would have to be a beginning and exclude eternity. Eternity is not appeased, because it does not have a subject that takes it upon itself.

One can also find this turning of nothingness into existing in Heidegger. The Heideggerian nothingness still has a sort of activity and being: "nothingness nothings."[21] It does not keep still. It affirms itself in this production of nothingness.

But if it were necessary to compare the notion of the *there is* with a great theme of classical philosophy, I would think of Heraclitus. Not to the myth of the river in which one cannot bathe twice, but to Cratylus' version of the river in which one cannot bathe even once;[22] where the very fixity of unity, the form of every existent, cannot be constituted; the river wherein the last element of fixity, in relation to which becoming is understood, disappears.

[21]This peculiar expression is found several times in Heidegger's 1929 article, "What is Metaphysics" (translated by R.F.C. Hull and A. Crick, found in *Existence and Being*, edited by W. Brock [Chicago: Henry Regnery Co., 1970], pp. 325–61). See also section 58 of *Being and Time*, "Understanding and Appeal and Guilt" (pp. 325–35), where Heidegger links nothingness and existence.

[22]For Cratylus' version of the Heraclitean river, see Aristotle, *Metaphysics*, IV, 1010a18. For a contemporary discussion of it, see G.S. Kirk, J. E. Raven, and M. Schofield, *The Presocratic Philosophers*, 2nd ed. (Cambridge University Press, 1983), pp. 195–96. Levinas again refers to Cratylus' river in *Totality and Infinity*, p. 60.

This existing without existents, which I call the *there is*, is the place where hypostasis will be produced.[23]

But first I want to stress at greater length the consequences of this conception of the *there is*. It consists in promoting a notion of being without nothingness, which leaves no hole and permits no escape. And this impossibility of nothingness deprives suicide, which is the final mastery one can have over being, of its function of mastery. One is no longer master of anything—that is, one is in the absurd. Suicide appears as the final recourse against the absurd.[24] I mean suicide in the broad sense of the term, also including the despairing yet lucid struggle of a Macbeth, who fights even when he has recognized the uselessness of combat.[25] This mastery, this possibility of finding a meaning for existence through the possibility of suicide, is a constant fact of tragedy. Juliette's cry in the third act of *Romeo and Juliette*—"I keep the power to die"—is still a triumph over fatality. One can say that tragedy, in general, is not simply the victory of fate over freedom, for through the death assumed at the moment of the alleged victory of fate the individual escapes fate. And it is for this reason that Hamlet is beyond tragedy or the tragedy of tragedy. He understands that the "not to be" is perhaps impossible and he can no longer master the absurd, even by suicide.[26] The notion of irremissible being, without exit, constitutes the fun-

[23]In *Totality and Infinity* Levinas writes: "The term 'production' designates both the effectuation of being (the event 'is produced,' an automobile 'is produced') and its being brought to light or its exposition (an argument 'is produced,' an actor 'is produced'). The ambiguity of this verb conveys the essential ambiguity of the operation by which the being of an entity simultaneously is brought about and is revealed" (p. 26). See also Lingis' footnote on the same page.

[24]Levinas doubtlessly has in mind the issues raised by Albert Camus in his popular 1942 text, *The Myth of Sisyphus* (translated by J. O'Brien [New York: Random House, 1959]).

[25]See pp. 71–73 below, "Death and the Future."

[26]Levinas again refers to suicide and Shakespeare's Hamlet in *Existence and Existents*, pp. 61–62; and *Totality and Infinity*, p. 231.

damental absurdity of being. Being is evil not because it is finite but because it is without limits. Anxiety, according to Heidegger, is the experience of nothingness.[27] Is it not, on the contrary—if by death one means nothingness—the fact that it is impossible to die?

It can also seem paradoxical to characterize the *there is* by vigilance, as if the pure event of existing were endowed with a consciousness. But it is necessary to ask if vigilance defines consciousness, or if consciousness is not indeed rather the possibility of tearing itself away from vigilance, if the proper meaning of consciousness does not consist in being a vigilance backed against a possibility of sleep, if the feat of the ego is not the power to leave the situation of impersonal vigilance. In fact, consciousness already participates in vigilance. But what characterizes it particularly is its always retaining the possibility of withdrawing "behind" to sleep. Consciousness is the power to sleep.[28] This leak within the plenum is the very paradox of consciousness.

HYPOSTASIS

Consciousness is a rupture of the anonymous vigilance of the *there is;* it is already hypostasis; it refers to a situation where an existent is put in touch with its existing. Obviously I will not be able to explain *why* this takes place. There is no physics in metaphysics. I can simply show what the significance of hypostasis is.[29]

The appearance of a "something that is" constitutes a

---

[27]Heidegger, *Being and Time*, pp. 233 and 321.

[28]Levinas returns to the connections between sleep, insomnia, and consciousness in *Existence and Existents*, pp. 65–71; and "God and Philosophy," pp. 129–30.

[29]On "hypostasis," see note 6, above.

veritable inversion at the heart of anonymous being. "Something that is" bears existing as an attribute, is master of this existing as the subject is master of an attribute. Existing is its own, and it is precisely through this mastery (whose limits we shall soon see), through this jealous and unshared mastery over existing, that the existent is alone. More exactly, the appearance of an existent is the very constitution of a mastery, of a freedom in an existing that by itself would remain fundamentally anonymous. In order for there to be an existent in this anonymous existing, it is necessary that a departure from self and a return to self—that is, that the very work of identity—become possible. Through its identification the existent is already closed up upon itself; it is a monad and a solitude.

The present is the event of hypostasis. The present leaves itself—better still, its *is* the departure from self. It is a rip in the infinite beginningless and endless fabric of existing. The present rips apart and joins together again; it begins; it is beginning itself. It has a past, but in the form of remembrance. It has a history, but it is not history.

Positing hypostasis as a present is still not to introduce time into being. Although giving us the present, we are given neither a stretch of time set within a linear series of duration, nor a point of this series. It is not a matter of a present cut out of a current, already constituted time, or of an element of time, but of the *function* of the present, of the rip that it brings about in the impersonal infinity of existing. It is like an ontological schema. On the one hand, it is an event and not yet something; it does not exist; but it is an event of existing through which something comes to start out from itself. On the other hand, it is still a pure event that must be expressed by a verb; and nonetheless there is a sort of molting in this existing, already a something, already an existent. It is essential to grasp the present at the limit of existing and the existent, where, in function of existing, it already turns into an existent.

This is precisely because the present is a way of accomplishing[30] the "starting out from itself" that is always an evanescence. If the present endured, it would have received its existence from something preceding. It would have benefited from a heritage. But it is something that comes from itself. One cannot come from oneself otherwise than by receiving nothing from the past. Evanescence would thus be the essential form of beginning.

But how can this evanescence result in something? By a dialectical situation that describes rather than excludes a phenomenon that is called for now: the "I."

Philosophers have always recognized the amphibolous character of the "I": it is not a substance, nevertheless it is preeminently an existent. To define it by spirituality says nothing if spirituality is equivalent to properties. It says nothing about its mode of existence, about the absolute that in the ego does not exclude a power of total renewal. To say that this power has an absolute existence is at least to transform this power into a substance. On the contrary, grasped at the limit of existing and the existent, as a function of hypostasis, the ego stands directly outside the oppositions of the variable and the permanent, as well as outside the categories of being and nothingness. The paradox ceases when one understands that the "I" is not initially an existent but a mode of existing itself, that properly speaking it does not exist. To be sure, the present and the "I" turn into existents, and one can form them into a time, so that they have time like an existent. And one can have a Kantian or Bergsonian experience of this hypostatized

[30]Like the term "production," Levinas has chosen the term "accomplish" carefully. In *Totality and Infinity*, with an eye to the limits of phenomenology, he writes: "The break-up of the formal structure of thought (the noema of a noesis) into events which this structure dissimulates, but which sustain it and restore its concrete significance, constitutes a *deduction*—necessary and yet non-analytical. In our exposition it is indicated by expressions such as "that is," or "precisely," or "this accomplishes that," or "this is produced as that," (p. 28).

time. But it is then the experience of a hypostatized time, a time that is. It is no longer time in its schematic function between existing and the existent, time as the pure event of hypostasis. In positing the present as the mastery of the existent over existing, and in seeking in it the passage from existing to the existent, we find ourselves at a level of investigation that can no longer be qualified as experience. And if phenomenology is only a method of radical experience, we will find ourselves beyond phenomenology. The hypostasis of the present, however, is only one moment of hypostasis; time can indicate another relationship between existing and the existent. This is what will later appear to us as the very event of our relationship with the Other, permitting us to conclude then with a pluralist existence surpassing the monist hypostasis of the present.

As present and "I," hypostasis is freedom. The existent is master of existing. It exerts on its existence the virile power of the subject. It has something in its power.

It is a first freedom—not yet the freedom of free will, but the freedom of beginning. It is by starting out from something now that there is existence. Freedom is included in every subject, in the very fact that there is a subject, that there is a being. It is the freedom of the existent in its very grip on existing.

SOLITUDE AND HYPOSTASIS

If solitude in this study has initially been characterized as the indissoluble unity between the existent and its existing, it thus does not result from some presupposition about the other. It does not appear as a privation of a previously given relationship with the Other. It results from the work of hypostasis. Solitude is the very unity of the existent, the fact that there is something in existing starting from which existence occurs. The subject is alone because it is one. A solitude is necessary in order for there to be a freedom of beginning, the existent's mastery over existing—that is, in brief, in order for there to be an existent. Solitude is thus not only a despair and an abandonment, but also a virility, a pride and a sovereignty. These are traits the existentialist analysis of solitude, pursued exclusively in terms of despair, has succeeded in effacing, making one forget all the themes of the Romantic and Byronic literature and psychology of proud, aristocratic and genial solitude.[31]

SOLITUDE AND MATERIALITY

But the subject's mastery over existing, the existent's sovereignty, involves a dialectical reversal.

Existing is mastered by the existent that is identical to itself—that is to say, alone. But identity is not only a departure from self; it is also a return to self. The present consists in an inevitable return to itself. The price paid for the existent's position lies in the very fact that it cannot detach itself from itself. The existent is occupied with itself [s'occuper de soi]. This manner of being occupied with itself is the subject's materiality. Identity is not an inoffensive relationship with itself, but an enchainment to itself; it is the necessity of being occupied with itself. Beginning is made heavy by itself; it is the present of being and not of a dream. Its freedom is immediately limited by its responsibility. This is its great paradox: a free being is already no longer free, because it is responsible for itself.

Though it is a freedom with regard to the past and fu-

---

[31]Levinas develops these analyses of the existent's primordial and irreducible independence and sovereignty in *Existence and Existents* (pp. 17-36) and *Totality and Infinity* (pp.110-14, 117-20, 127-40, 144-51). Even though, as we shall see, the existent's solitude turns out to be insufficient (for its needs) and inferior (to ethical-social life), Levinas is emphasizing here that it ought not therefore to be understood solely in terms of what it *lacks*. The existent *is* separate, come what may.

ture, the present is an enchainment in relation to itself. The material character of the present does not result from the fact that the past weighs upon it or that it is anxious about its future.[32] It results from the present as present. The present has torn the fabric of infinite existing; it ignores history; it comes starting out from now. And despite this or because of this, it commits itself and through this knows a responsibility, turns into materiality.

In psychological and anthropological descriptions this is explained by the fact that the I is already riveted to itself, its freedom is not as light as grace but already a heaviness, the ego is irremissably itself. I am not dramatizing a tautology. The turning of the ego back upon itself is precisely neither a serene reflection nor the result of a purely philosophical reflection. The relationship with itself is, as in Blanchot's novel *Aminadab*,[33] the relationship with a double chained to the ego, a viscous, heavy, stupid double, but one the ego [*le moi*] is with precisely because it is me [*moi*]. This *with* is manifest in the fact that it is necessary to be occupied with oneself. Every undertaking is a sort of domestic stirring. I do not exist as a spirit, or as a smile or a breath of air; I am not without responsibility. My being doubles with a having; I am encumbered by myself. And this is material existence. Consequently, materiality does not express the contingent fall of the spirit into the tomb or prison of a body. Materiality accompanies—necessarily—the upsurge of the subject in its existent freedom. To understand the body starting with its materiality—the concrete event of the relationship between Ego [*Moi*] and Self [*Soi*]—is to reduce it to an ontological event. Ontological relationships are not disembodied ties. The relationship between Ego and Self is

[32]On the anxiety of the future in Heidegger, see *Being and Time*, pp. 306–11; on the weight of the past, pp. 329–34. In Sartre, see "Phenomenology of the Three Temporal Dimensions" in *Being and Nothingness*, translated by H. Barnes (New York: Washington Square Press, 1969) pp. 159–87.

[33]Maurice Blanchot, *Aminadab* (Paris: Gallimard, 1942).

not an inoffensive reflection of the spirit upon itself. It is the whole of human materiality.

The freedom of the Ego and its materiality thus go together. The first freedom resultant from the fact that in anonymous existing an existent arises, includes as its price the very finality of the *I* riveted to itself. This finality of the existent, which constitutes the tragedy of solitude, is materiality. Solitude is not tragic because it is the privation of the other, but because it is shut up within the captivity of its identity, because it is matter. To shatter the enchainment of matter is to shatter the finality of hypostasis. It is to be in time. Solitude is an absence of time. The time *given*, itself hypostatized and studied, the time the subject travels by carrying its identity, is a time incapable of loosening the tie of hypostasis.

[PART II]

Matter is the misfortune [*malheur*] of hypostasis. Materiality and solitude go together. Solitude is not a higher-level anxiety that is revealed to a being when all its needs are satisfied It is not the privileged experience of *being toward death*, but the companion, so to speak, of an everyday existence haunted by matter. And to the extent that material concerns issue from hypostasis itself and express the very event of our existent freedom, everyday life, far from constituting a fall, and far from appearing as a betrayal with regard to our metaphysical destiny, emanates from our solitude and forms the very accomplishment of solitude and the infinitely serious attempt to respond to its profound unhappiness [*malheur*]. Everyday life is a preoccupation with salvation.

EVERYDAY LIFE AND SALVATION

Can one not thus resolve a contradiction that all contemporary philosophy plays out? The hope for a better society and the despair of solitude, both of which are founded on experiences that claim to be self-evident, seem to be in an insurmountable antagonism. There is not merely an opposition but an antinomy between the experience of solitude and social experience. Each of them claims the rank of a universal experience and manages to account for the other, referring to it particularly as the degradation of an authentic experience.

The feeling of solitude persists and threatens in the very midst of the optimistic constructivism of sociology and socialism. It enables one to denounce the joys of communication, collective works, and everything that makes the world livable, as Pascalian diversion and the simple forgetfulness of solitude. The fact of finding oneself settled in the world, occupied with things, attached to them, and even the aspiration to dominate them, is not merely depreciated in the experience of solitude, but explained by a philosophy of solitude. Concern for things and needs would be a fall, a flight before the uttermost finality[34] that these needs themselves imply, an inconsequence, a nontruth, inevitable, to be sure, but bearing the mark of the inferior and the reprehensible.

But the inverse is equally true. We behave like the frightful bourgeois in the midst of Pascalian, Kierkegaardian, Nietzschean, and Heideggerian anxieties. Or we are crazy. No one will recommend madness as a way of salvation. The buffoon, the fool of Shakespearean tragedy, is the one who feels and bespeaks with lucidity the unsubstantiality of the world and the absurdity of its situations—the one who is not the principal character of tragedy, the one who has nothing to overcome. In a world of kings, princes, and heroes, the fool is the opening through which this world is swept by drafts of madness; the fool is not the tempest that extinguishes the lights and tears away the curtains. However much the entirety of preoccupations that fill our days and tear us away from solitude to throw us into contact with our peers are called "fall," "everyday life," "animality," "degradation," or "base materialism," these preoccupations are in any case in no way frivolous. One can think

<hr/>

[34]For Heidegger *Dasein* usually lives in the possibilities that permit it to flee from an authentic awareness of death, its uttermost [*ausserst*] possibility; indeed, inauthentic everyday life is constituted by flight from death. See Heidegger, *Being and Time*, pp. 294, 297–99.

that authentic time is originally an ecstasis,[35] yet one buys oneself a watch; despite the nudity of existence, one must as far as possible be decently clothed. And when one writes a book on anxiety, one writes it for someone, one goes through all the steps that separate the draft from the publication, and one sometimes behaves like a merchant of anxiety. The man condemned to die straightens out his uniform before his last walk, accepts a final cigarette, and finds an eloquent word before the salvo.

These may seem like facile objections, recalling the ones certain realists address to idealists when they reproach them for eating and breathing in an illusory world. But under the circumstances they are less negligible objections: they do not oppose a behavior to a metaphysics but a behavior to a morality. Each of these antagonistic experiences is a morality. They object not to the error but to the inauthenticity of one another. There is something other than naivety in the flat denial the masses oppose to the elites when they are worried more about bread than about anxiety. From this comes the accent of greatness that stirs in a humanism springing from the economic problem; from this comes the very power that the demands of the working

[35]The notion of temporal "ecstasis" is central to all contemporary theories of time, especially those of Husserl and Heidegger, and their successors. It expresses the temporal character of the transcendence or the being-in-the-world of human existence (see note 2, above).

See Edmund Husserl, The Phenomenology of Internal Time-Consciousness, edited by M. Heidegger, translated by J. S. Churchill (Bloomington: Indiana University Press, 1971); Heidegger, Being and Time, p. 377 and passim; and Heidegger, "Letter on Humanism," translated by F. A. Capuzzi, in Basic Writings, edited by D. F. Krell (New York: Harper & Row, 1977) pp. 193–242.

Much secondary literature has appeared on the ecstasis of time in Heidegger and Husserl. For one good account of time in Husserl, see Robert Sokolowski's "The Inside of Time" in Husserlian Meditations (Evanston: Northwestern University Press, 1974), pp. 138–68; for Heidegger (and Husserl), see the chapter on "Temporality" in Maurice Merleau-Ponty's The Phenomenology of Perception, translated by C. Smith (London: Routledge & Kegan Paul, 1962), especially pp. 418–22.

class possess to be elevated into a humanism. They would be inexplicable for a behavior that was to have been simply a fall into inauthenticity, or likewise a diversion, or even a legitimate exigency of our animality.

For a constructive and optimistic socialism, however, solitude and its anxieties are an ostrichlike position in a world that solicits solidarity and lucidity; they are epiphenomena—phenomena of luxury or waste—of a period of social transformation, the senseless dream of an eccentric individual, a luxation in the collective body. And it is with a right equal to that used by the philosophy of solitude that the anxiety of death and solitude can be called by socialist humanism "falsehood" and "idle chatter," and even "mystification" and "deceptive eloquence," "flight before the essential" and "deliquescence."

This antinomy opposes the need to be saved and the need to be satisfied—Jacob and Esau. But the true relationship between salvation and satisfaction is not that which classic idealism perceived, and that despite everything modern existentialism maintains. Salvation does not require the satisfaction of need, like a higher principle that would require the solidity of its bases to be secured. The daily run of our everyday life is surely not a simple sequel of our animality continually surpassed by spiritual activity. But neither does the anxiety about salvation arise in suffering a need that would be its occasional cause, as if poverty or the proletarian condition were the occasion for glimpsing the gate of the Heavenly Kingdom. I do not believe that the oppression that crushes the working classes gives it uniquely a pure experience of oppression in order to awaken in it, beyond economic liberation, the nostalgia for a metaphysical liberation. The revolutionary struggle is divested of its true significance and its real intention when it serves simply as a basis for spiritual life, or when through its crises it must awaken vocations. Economic struggle is already on an equal footing with the struggle for salvation because it is founded in the very dialectic of hypostasis through which the first freedom is constituted.

In Sartre's philosophy there is some sort of angelical present. The whole weight of existence being thrown back onto the past, the freedom of the present is already situated above matter. In recognizing the whole weight of matter in the present itself and in its emerging freedom, we want both to recognize material life and its triumph over the anonymity of existing, and the tragic finality to which it is bound by its very freedom.

By connecting solitude to the subject's materiality—materiality being its enchainment to itself—we can understand in what sense the world and our existence in the world constitute a fundamental advance of the subject in overcoming the weight that it is to itself, in overcoming it's materiality—that is to say, in loosening the bond between the self and the ego.

SALVATION THROUGH THE WORLD—NOURISHMENTS

In everyday existence, in the world, the material structure of the subject is to a certain extent overcome: an interval appears between the ego and the self. The identical subject does not return to itself immediately.

Since Heidegger we are in the habit of considering the world as an ensemble of tools.[36] Existing in the world is acting, but acting in such a way that in the final account action has our own existence for its object. Tools refer to one another to finally refer to our care for existing.[37] In turning on

[36]For Heidegger practice precedes theory and is the initial and implicit realm of significance; see Heidegger, *Being and Time*, sections 14 and 15.

[37]In *Being and Time* Heidegger distinguishes three levels: *Dasein*'s "concern" *(Besorgen)* for things within the world; *Dasein*'s "solicitude" *(Fürsorge)* for other persons within the world; and *Dasein*'s "care" *(Sorge)* for being-in-the-world as such—that is, its care for itself qua *Da-sein*. It is no

a bathroom switch we open up the entire ontological problem. What seems to have escaped Heidegger—if it is true that in these matters something might have escaped Heidegger—is that prior to being a system of tools, the world is an ensemble of nourishments. Human life in the world does not go beyond the objects that fulfil it. It is perhaps not correct to say that we live to eat, but it is no more correct to say that we eat to live. The uttermost finality of eating is contained in food. When one smells a flower, it is the smell that limits the finality of the act. To stroll is to enjoy the fresh air, not for health but for the air. These are the nourishments characteristic of our existence in the world. It is an ecstatic existence—being outside oneself—but limited by the object.

This relationship with an object can be characterized by enjoyment [*jouissance*]. All enjoyment is a way of being, but also a sensation—that is, light and knowledge. It is absorption of the object, but also distance with regard to it. Knowledge and luminosity essentially belong to enjoying. Through this, before the nourishments that offer themselves, the subject is in space, at a distance from all the objects that are necessary for its existence. Though in the pure and simple identity of hypostasis, the subject is bogged down in itself, in the world, instead of a return to itself, there is a "relationship with everything that is necessary for being." The subject separates from itself. Light is the prerequisite for such a possibility. In this sense our everyday life is already a way of being free from the initial materiality through which a subject is accomplished [*s'accomplit*]. It al-

accident that the latter, care—*Sorge*—is etymologically and ontologically at the root of the other two. The "call of care" draws *Dasein* from out of its ordinary (= within-the-world) absorption with things and persons to an authentic relationship with itself. It is to this ultimate reflexivity that Levinas is here alluding. See Heidegger, *Being and Time*, pp. 116–17 (on the referral from tool use to *Dasein*); 332–34, 341–45 (on the general structure of ultimate referral to *Dasein*).

ready contains a forgetfulness of self. The morality of
"earthly nourishments" is the first morality, the first abnegation. It is not the last, but one must pass through it.[38]

THE TRANSCENDENCE OF LIGHT AND REASON

Self-forgetfulness and the luminosity of enjoyment do not
break the irremissible attachment of the ego to the self
when one separates this light from the ontological event of
the subject's materiality, where it has its place, and when,
in the name of reason, one elevates this light into an absolute. The interval of space given by light is instantaneously
absorbed by light. Light is that through which something is
other than myself, but already as if it came from me. The illuminated object is something one encounters, but from
the very fact that it is illuminated one encounters it as if it
came from us.[39] It does not have a fundamental strange-

[38]Levinas: This conception of enjoyment as a departure from the self is
opposed to Platonism. Plato makes a calculation when he denounces the
mixed pleasures; they are impure since they presuppose a lack that is
filled without any real gain being recorded. But it is not right to judge enjoyment in terms of profits and losses. One must view it in its becoming,
its event, in relationship to the drama of the ego inscribed in being,
thrown into a dialectic. The entire attraction of earthly nourishments and
the entire experience of youth is opposed to Platonic calculation.
   [The notion of enjoyment—prior to theory and practice—is developed in
Existence and Existents, pp. 37–45; *Totality and Infinity*, pp. 127–39, 143–51;
and *Otherwise than Being*, pp. 72–74. See also, R. Cohen, "Emmanuel
Levinas: Happiness is a Sensational Time," *Philosophy Today*, vol. 25, no. 3
(Fall 1981), pp. 196–203.]

[39]Levinas: I take this opportunity to return to a point treated here at this
college by Alphonse de Waelhens in his fine lecture. It is a question of
Husserl. De Waelhens reckons that the reason that prompted Husserl to
shift from descriptive intuition to transcendental analysis resulted from an
identification of intelligibility and construction—pure vision not being intelligibility. I think, to the contrary, that the Husserlian notion of vision already implies intelligibility. To see is already to render the encountered
object one's own, as drawn from one's own ground. In this sense, "transcendental constitution" is but a way of seeing in full clarity. It is a completion of vision.

ness. Its transcendence is wrapped in immanence. The exteriority of light does not suffice for the liberation of the ego that is the self's captive.

Light and knowledge appeared to us in their place in hypostasis and in the dialectic it brings forth, as a way for the subject—emancipated from the anonymity of existing but riveted to itself through its identity as an existent (that is, materialized)—to take a distance with regard to its materiality. But separated from this ontological event, separated from the materiality that is promised other dimensions of liberation, knowledge does not surmount solitude. By themselves reason and light consummate the solitude of a being as a being, and accomplish its destiny to be the sole and unique point of reference for everything.

By encompassing everything within its universality, reason finds itself once again in solitude. Solipsism is neither an aberration nor a sophism; it is the very structure of reason. This is so not just because of the "subjective" character of the sensations that it combines, but because of the universality of knowledge—that is, the unlimitedness of light and the impossibility for anything to be on the outside.[40] Thus reason never finds any other reason to speak. The intentionality of consciousness allows one to distinguish the ego from things, but it does not make solipsism disappear: its element—light—renders us master of the exterior world but is incapable of discovering a peer for us there. The objectivity of rational knowledge removes nothing of the solitary character of reason. The possible reversal of objectivity into subjectivity is the very theme of idealism,

[40] The final chapter of *Otherwise than Being or Beyond Essence* is entitled simply "Outside."

[See A. Lingis, "On Phenomenological Explanation," *The Journal of the British Society for Phenomenology*, vol. 11, no. 1 (January 1980), pp. 54–68; reprinted in A. Lingis, *Phenomenological Explanations* (Dordrecht: Martinus Nijhoff, 1986) pp. 1–19.]

which is a philosophy of reason. Subjectivity is itself the objectivity of light. Every object can be spoken of in terms of consciousness—that is, can be brought to light.

The reality of the transcendence of space could be secured only if it is founded on a transcendence without a return to its point of departure. Life could only become the path of redemption if, in its struggle with matter, it encounters an event that stops its everyday transcendence from falling back upon a point that is always the same. To catch sight of this transcendence, which supports the transcendence of light and lends a real exteriority to the exterior world, it is necessary to return to the concrete situation wherein light is given in enjoyment—that is, to material existence.[41]

---

[41]The sequence of ideas followed here is also followed in *Existence and Existents*: a section on light (pp. 46–51) comes after the section on enjoyment (see note 38, above). Also on light, see *Totality and Infinity*, pp. 189 and passim.

[PART III]

I have dealt with the subject alone, alone due to the very fact that it is an existent. The solitude of the subject results from its relationship with the existing over which it is master. This mastery over existing is the power of beginning, of starting out from itself, starting out from itself neither to act nor to think, but to be.

I then showed that liberation with regard to the existent's anonymous existing becomes an enchainment to self, the very enchainment of identification. Concretely, the relationship of identification is the encumbrance of the ego by the self, the care that the ego takes of itself, or materiality. The subject—an abstraction from every relationship with a future or with a past—is thrust upon itself, and is so in the very freedom of its present. Its solitude is not initially the fact that it is without succor, but its being thrown into feeding upon itself, its being mired in itself. This is materiality. So in the very instant of the transcendence of need, placing the subject in front of nourishments, in front of the world as nourishment, this transcendence offers the subject a liberation from itself. The world offers the subject participation in existing in the form of enjoyment, and consequently permits it to exist at a distance from itself. The subject is absorbed in the object it absorbs, and nevertheless keeps a distance with regard to that object. All enjoyment is also sensation—that is, knowledge and light. It is not just the disappearance of the self, but self-forgetfulness, as a first abnegation.

WORK

But this instantaneous transcendence through space does not manage to escape solitude. The light that permits encountering something other than the self, makes it encountered as if this thing came from the ego. The light, brightness, is intelligibility itself; making everything come from me, it reduces every experience to an element of reminiscence. Reason is alone. And in this sense knowledge never encounters anything truly other in the world. This is the profound truth of idealism. It betokens a radical difference between spatial exteriority and the exteriority of instants in relation to one another.

In the concreteness of need, the space that keeps us away from ourselves is always to be conquered. One must cross it and take hold of an object—that is, one must work with one's hands. In this sense, "the one who works not, eats not" is an analytic proposition. Tools and the manufacture of tools pursue the chimerical ideal of the suppression of distances. In the perspective that opens upon the tool, beginning with the modern tool—the machine—one is much more struck by its function which consists in suppressing work, than by its instrumental function, which Heidegger exclusively considered.

In work—meaning, in effort, in its pain and sorrow—the subject finds the weight of the existence which involves its existent freedom itself. Pain and sorrow are the phenomena to which the solitude of the existent is finally reduced.

SUFFERING AND DEATH[42]

In pain, sorrow, and suffering, we once again find, in a state of purity, the finality that constitutes the tragedy of

[42]The themes of this section are taken up and developed in the section entitled "Time and the Will: Patience," in *Totality and Infinity*, pp. 236–40.

solitude. The ecstasis of enjoyment does not succeed in surmounting this finality. Two points must be emphasized: I am going to pursue the analysis of solitude in the pain of need and work, not in the anxiety of nothingness; and I am going to lay stress on the pain lightly called physical, for in it engagement in existence is without any equivocation. While in moral pain one can preserve an attitude of dignity and compunction, and consequently already be free; physical suffering in all its degrees entails the impossibility of detaching oneself from the instant of existence. It is the very irremissibility of being. The content of suffering merges with the impossibility of detaching oneself from suffering. And this is not to define suffering by suffering, but to insist on the *sui generis* implication that constitutes its essence. In suffering there is an absence of all refuge. It is the fact of being directly exposed to being. It is made up of the impossibility of fleeing or retreating. The whole acuity of suffering lies in this impossibility of retreat. It is the fact of being backed up against life and being. In this sense suffering is the impossibility of nothingness.

But in suffering there is, at the same time as the call to an impossible nothingness, the proximity of death. There is not only the feeling and the knowledge that suffering can end in death. Pain of itself includes it like a paroxysm, as if there were something about to be produced even more rending than suffering, as if despite the entire absence of a dimension of withdrawal that constitutes suffering, it still had some free space for an event, as if it must still get uneasy about something, as if we were on the verge of an event beyond what is revealed to the end in suffering. The structure of pain, which consists in its very attachment to pain, is prolonged further, but up to an unknown that is impossible to translate into terms of light—that is, that is refractory to the intimacy of the self with the ego to which all our experiences return. The unknown of death, which is not given straight off as nothingness but is correlative to an experience of the impossibility of nothingness, signifies not that death is a region from which no one has returned and consequently remains unknown as a matter of fact; the unknown of death signifies that the very relationship with death cannot take place in the light, that the subject is in relationship with what does not come from itself. We could say it is in relationship with mystery.

This way death has of announcing itself in suffering, outside all light, is an experience of the passivity of the subject, which until then had been active and remained active even when it was overwhelmed by its own nature, but reserved its possibility of assuming its factual state. To say "an experience of passivity" is only a way of speaking, for experience always already signifies knowledge, light, and initiative, as well as the return of the object to the subject. Death as mystery contrasts strongly with experience thus understood. In knowledge all passivity is activity through the intermediary of light. The object that I encounter is understood and, on the whole, constructed by me, even though death announces an event over which the subject is not master, an event in relation to which the subject is no longer a subject.

I at once take note of what this analysis of death in suffering presents that is unusual, in relation to the celebrated Heideggerian analyses of *being toward death*. Being toward death, in Heidegger's authentic existence, is a supreme lucidity and hence a supreme virility. It is *Dasein*'s assumption of the uttermost possibility of existence, which precisely makes possible all other possibilities,[43] and consequently makes possible the very feat of grasping a possibility—that is, it makes possible activity and freedom. Death in Heidegger is an event of freedom, whereas for me the subject seems to reach the limit of the possible in suf-

[43]Levinas: Death in Heidegger is not, as Jean Wahl says "the impossibility of possibility," but "the possibility of impossibility." [See Heidegger, *Being and Time*, pp. 294, 307.] This apparently Byzantine distinction has a fundamental importance. [See *Totality and Infinity*, p. 235.]

fering. It finds itself enchained, overwhelmed, and in some way passive. Death is in this sense the limit of idealism.

I even wonder how the principal trait of our relationship with death could have escaped philosophers' attention. It is not with the nothingness of death, of which we precisely know nothing, that the analysis must begin, but with the situation where something absolutely unknowable appears. Absolutely unknowable means foreign to all light, rendering every assumption of possibility impossible, but where we ourselves are seized.

DEATH AND THE FUTURE[44]

This is why death is never a present.[45] This is a truism. The ancient adage designed to dissipate the fear of death— "If you are, it is not; if it is, you are not"[46]—without doubt misunderstands the entire paradox of death, for it effaces our relationship with death, which is a unique relationship with the future. But at least the adage insists on the eternal futurity of death. The fact that it deserts every present is not due to our evasion[47] of death and to an unpardonable

[44] The themes of this section are later taken up and developed in *Totality and Infinity*, in the section entitled "The Will and Death" (pp. 232-236), which directly precedes—rather than follows—the section of *Totality and Infinity* indicated in note 42 above, thus reversing the order of development found in *Time and the Other*.

[45] "Present" in English and French can mean either the present time or a gift. As this section will show, the emphasis is on the former, the temporal meaning.

[46] Epicurus, Letter to Menoeceus.

[47] The earliest published text containing what is perhaps the nascent kernal of Levinas' thought—hidden within the husks of Heideggerian ontology—is entitled "De l'évasion" ["On Evasion"] (*Recherches philosophiques*, vol. 5 [1935/36] pp. 373-92); republished as a book (Montepellier: Fata Morgana, 1982) introduced and annotated by J. Rolland). Its main theme is the escape of the self from its enchainment with itself. It is noteworthy, furthermore, in that it contains, nearly three years before the publication of Sartre's famous novel *Nausea*, several pages describing "the very experience of pure being" in terms of the experience of nausea!

diversion at the supreme hour, but to the fact that death is *ungraspable*, that it marks the end of the subject's virility and heroism. The now is the fact that I am master, master of the possible, master of grasping the possible. Death is never now. When death is here, I am no longer here, not just because I am nothingness, but because I am unable to grasp. My mastery, my virility, my heroism as a subject can be neither virility nor heroism in relation to death. There is in the suffering at the heart of which we have grasped this nearness of death—and still at the level of the phenomenon—this reversal of the subject's activity into passivity. This is not just in the instant of suffering where, backed against being, I still grasp it and am still the subject of suffering, but in the crying and sobbing toward which suffering is inverted. Where suffering attains its purity, where there is no longer anything between us and it, the supreme responsibility of this extreme assumption turns into supreme irresponsibility, into infancy. Sobbing is this, and precisely through this it announces death. To die is to return to this state of irresponsibility, to be the infantile shaking of sobbing.

Allow me to return once again to Shakespeare, in whom I have overindulged in the course of these lectures. But it sometimes seems to me that the whole of philosophy is only a meditation of Shakespeare. Does not the hero of tragedy assume death? I will allow myself a very brief analysis of Macbeth's end. Macbeth learns that Birnam Wood marches on the castle of Dunsinane, and is the sign of defeat: death approaches. When this sign comes true, Macbeth says: "Blow wind! come, wrack!" But right afterward: "Ring the alarm-bell! [etc. . . .] At least we'll die with harness on our back." Prior to death there will be battle. The second sign of defeat has not yet come about. Had not the witches predicted that a man of woman born could do nothing against Macbeth? But here is Macduff, who was not of woman born. Death is coming now. "Accursed by that tongue that tells," cries Macbeth to Macduff who learns of his power over him, "for it hath cow'd my better part of man!...I'll not fight with thee."

This is the passivity when there is no longer hope. This is what I have called the "end of virility." But immediately hope is reborn, and here are Macbeth's last words: "Though Birnam Wood be come to Dunsinane, and thou oppos'd, being of no woman born, yet I will try the last."

Prior to death there is always a last chance; this is what heroes seize, not death. The hero is the one who always glimpses a last chance, the one who obstinately finds chances. Death is thus never assumed, it comes. Suicide is a contradictory concept. The eternal immanence of death is part of its essence. In the present, where the subject's mastery is affirmed, there is hope. Hope is not added to death by a sort of *salto mortale*,[48] by a sort of inconsequence; it is in the very margin that is given, at the moment of death, to the subject who is going to die. *Spiro/spero*.[49] *Hamlet* is precisely a lengthy testimony to this impossibility of assuming death. Nothingness is impossible. It is nothingness that would have left humankind the possibility of assuming death and snatching a supreme mastery from out of the servitude of existence. "To be or not to be"[50] is a sudden awareness of this impossibility of annihilating oneself.

[48]A somersault [literally: "deadly-jump"]. This expression reappears in *Totality and Infinity*, p. 246.

[49]["If] I breathe, I hope."

[50]In English in original. Jankelevitch also protests against this seemingly all-inclusive disjunction; see the section entitled "Etre ou n'être pas?" [To be or not to be?"] in his *Philosophie Première* (Paris: Presses Universitaires de France, 1954), pp. 36–38.

Almost thirty-five years after *Time and the Other*, Levinas again recalls Hamlet's famous question in "Bad Conscience and the Inexorable," where he writes: "To be or not to be—this is probably not the question par excellence" (in *Face to Face with Levinas*, edited by R. Cohen [Albany: State University of New York Press, 1986], p. 40).

The Event And The Other [L'Autre]

What can we infer from this analysis of death? Death becomes the limit of the subject's virility, the virility made possible by the hypostasis at the heart of anonymous being, and manifest in the phenomenon of the present, in the light. It is not just that there exist ventures impossible for the subject, that its powers are in some way finite; death does not announce a reality against which nothing can be done, against which our power is insufficient—realities exceeding our strength already arise in the world of light. What is important about the approach of death is that at a certain moment we are no longer *able to be able* [*nous ne 'pouvons plus pouvoir'*].[51] It is exactly thus that the subject loses its very mastery as a subject.

This end of mastery indicates that we have assumed existing in such a way that an *event* can happen to us that we no longer assume, not even in the way we assume events—because we are always immersed in the empirical world—through vision. An event happens to us without our having absolutely anything "a priori," without our being able to have the least project, as one says today. Death is the impossibility of having a project. This approach of death indicates that we are in relation with something that is absolutely other, something bearing alterity not as a provisional determination we can assimilate through enjoyment, but as something whose very existence is made of alterity. My solitude is thus not confirmed by death but broken by it.

[51]The verb *pouvoir* means "to be able" or "can"; the noun means "power," "force," "means." Levinas' idea seems to be that in the face of the mystery of death, the subject not only loses its various powers, it loses its very ability to have powers, its "I can"—that is to say, its very self-constitution as an existent.

In his translation of Levinas' *Totality and Infinity*, Alphonso Lingis also notes this peculiar doubling of the verb *pouvoir* (pp. 39, 198, 236).

Right away this means that existence is pluralist. Here the plural is not a multiplicity of existents; it appears in existing itself. A plurality insinuates itself into the very existing of the existent, which until this point was jealously assumed by the subject alone and manifest through suffering. In death the existing of the existent is alienated. To be sure, the other [*l'Autre*] that is announced does not possess this existing as the subject possesses it; its hold over my existing is mysterious. It is not unknown but unknowable, refractory to all light. But this precisely indicates that the other is in no way another myself, participating with me in a common existence.[52] The relationship with the other is not an idyllic and harmonious relationship of communion, or a sympathy[53] through which we put ourselves in the other's place; we recognize the other as resembling us, but exterior to us; the relationship with the other is a relationship with a Mystery. The other's entire being is constituted by its

[52]Although Levinas is explicitly discussing the encounter with the alterity of death, this sentence and the ones following it conjure up the encounter with the alterity of the other person. What is common to death and social life is an encounter with radical alterity.

This important shift from solitude to social life, evinced by death, does not result, therefore, from an intellectual confusion or a fallaciously employed ambiguity. As will soon become clear (see especially the penultimate paragraph of the next section below), and as Levinas says unequivocally in *Totality and Infinity*, the encounter with the alterity of death is like nothing so much as the encounter with the alterity of the other person, "as though the approach of death remained one of the modalities of the relationship with the Other" (*TI*, p. 234).

It is alterity, then, not shared attributes, that is the key to social life.

In the above critical sentence, Levinas doubtlessly has in mind the alternative version of social life expressed in particular by Heidegger's notion of *mitsein* (previously mentioned) and Husserl's notion of "associative pairing," found in the fifth meditation of Edmund Husserl's *Cartesian Meditations* (translated by D. Cairns [The Hague: Martinus Nijhoff, 1970], pp. 89–151), a text that Levinas, along with Gabrielle Pfeiffer, translated into French for publication in 1931. (It is relevant, then, to note that Pfeiffer translated the first three meditations and Levinas translated the longer and final two meditations as well as Husserl's brief conclusion.)

[53]See Max Scheler, *The Nature of Sympathy*, translated by P. Heath (New Haven: Yale University Press, 1954); first German edition published in 1913, the second in 1923.

exteriority, or rather its alterity, for exteriority is a property of space and leads the subject back to itself through light.

Consequently only a being whose solitude has reached a crispation through suffering, and in relation with death, takes its place on a ground where the relationship with the other becomes possible. The relationship with the other will never be the feat of grasping a possibility. One would have to characterize it in terms that contrast strongly with the relationships that describe light. I think the erotic relationship furnishes us with a prototype of it. Eros, strong as death,[54] will furnish us with the basis of an analysis of this relationship with mystery—provided it is set forth in terms entirely different from those of the Platonism that is a world of light.

But it is possible to infer from this situation of death, where the subject no longer has any possibility of grasping, another characteristic of existence with the other. The future is what is in no way grasped. The exteriority of the future is totally different from spatial exteriority precisely through the fact that the future is absolutely surprising. Anticipation of the future and projection of the future, sanctioned as essential to time by all theories from Bergson[55] to Sartre, are but the present of the future and

---

[54] "*L'Eros, fort comme la mort . . . .*" This expression is found in the Song of Songs, 8:6. Franz Rosenzweig begins part 2, book 2, of *The Star of Redemption* with it; Lev Shestov refers to it in his 1937 book, *Athens and Jerusalem* (translated by B. Martin [New York: Simon and Schuster, 1968], p. 144).

[55] It is perhaps curious that Levinas includes Bergson here (as he does, similarly, in *Existence and Existents*, p. 94). Levinas often acknowledges his indebtedness to Bergson, who was, after all, *the* dominate French thinker at the beginning of the twentieth century, and led the way in rethinking time and its insertion of newness into being.

It was Bergson who argued, against previous notions of time (and proleptically against Heidegger's notion of time), that we must "succeed in conceiving the radically new and unforeseeable," which means rejecting the idea of " 'possibles' outlined beforehand . . . as if the will was limited to 'bringing about' one of them" (Henri Bergson, *The Creative Mind*, translated by M. Andison [New York: Philosophical Library, 1945], pp. 18–19).

In the opening comments and the third section of IV, below, Levinas will give his reasons for criticizing Bergson in this regard.

not the authentic future; the future is what is not grasped, what befalls us and lays hold of us. The other is the future. The very relationship with the other is the relationship with the future. It seems to me impossible to speak of time in a subject alone, or to speak of a purely personal duration.

OTHER AND THE OTHER[56]

I have just shown the possibility of an event in death. And I have contrasted this possibility, where the subject is no longer master of the event, with the possibility of the object, which the subject always masters and with which it is, in short, always alone. I have characterized this event as mystery, precisely because it could not be anticipated—that is, grasped; it could not enter into a present or it could enter into it as what does not enter it. But the death thus announced as other, as the alienation of my existence, is it still *my* death? If it opens a way out of solitude, does it not simply come to crush this solitude, to crush subjectivity itself? In death there is indeed an abyss between the event and the subject to whom it will happen. How can the event that cannot be grasped still happen to me? What can the other's relationship with a being, an existent, be? How can the existent exist as mortal and nonetheless persevere in its "personality," preserve its conquest over the anonymous "there is," its subject's mastery, the conquest of its subjectivity? How can a being enter into relation with the other without allowing its very self to be crushed by the other?

This question must be posed first, because it is the very problem of the preservation of the ego in transcendence. If the escape from solitude is meant to be something other than the absorption of the ego in the term toward which it

[56]*Autre et autrui.*

is projected, and if, on the other hand, the subject cannot assume death, as it assumes an object, how can this reconciliation between the ego and death come about? How, too, can the ego assume death without meanwhile assuming it as a possibility? If in the face of death one is no longer able to be able, how can one still remain a self before the event it announces?

The same problem is implied in a description faithful to the very phenomenon of death. The pathos of suffering does not consist solely in the impossibility of fleeing existing, of being backed up against it, but also in the terror of leaving this relationship of light whose transcendence death announces. Like Hamlet we prefer this known existence to unknown existence. It is as though the adventure into which the existent has entered by hypostasis were its sole recourse, its sole refuge against what is intolerable in that adventure. In death there is Lucretius' temptation of nothingness, and Pascal's desire for eternity.[57] These are not two distinct attitudes: we want both to die and to be.

The problem does not consist in rescuing an eternity from the jaws of death, but in allowing it to be welcomed, keeping for the ego—in the midst of an existence where an event happens to it—the freedom acquired by hypostasis. Such is the situation one can call the attempt to vanquish death, where at one time the event happens and yet the subject, without welcoming it, as one welcomes a thing or object, faces up to the event.

I have just described a dialectical situation. I am now going to show a concrete situation where this dialectic is accomplished. It is impossible for me to explain this method at length here; I have resorted to it again and again. One sees in any event that it is not phenomenological to the end.

The relationship with the Other, the face-to-face with the Other, the encounter with a face that at once gives and con-

[57]See Lucretius, *The Way Things Are*, book 3; Blaise Pascal, *Pensées*, passim.

ceals the Other, is the situation in which an event happens to a subject who does not assume it, who is utterly unable in its regard, but where nonetheless in a certain way it is in front of the subject. The other "assumed" is the Other.

TIME AND THE OTHER[58]

I hope to be able to show that the relationship with the Other is as entirely different from what the existentialists propose as it is from what the Marxists propose. For the moment I would like to at least indicate how time itself refers to this situation of the face-to-face with the Other.

The future that death gives, the future of the event, is not yet time. In order for this future, which is nobody's and which a human being cannot assume, to become an element of time, it must also enter into relationship with the present. What is the tie between two instants that have between them the whole interval, the whole abyss, that separates the present and death, this margin at once both insignificant and infinite, where there is always room enough for hope? It is certainly not a relationship of pure contiguity, which would transform time into space, but neither is it the élan of dynamism and duration, since for the present this power to be beyond itself and to encroach upon the future seems to me precisely excluded by the very mystery of death.

Relationship with the future, the presence of the future in the present, seems all the same accomplished in the face-to-face with the Other. The situation of the face-to-face would be the very accomplishment of time; the encroachment of the present on the future is not the feat of the subject alone, but the intersubjective relationship. The condition of time lies in the relationship between humans, or in history.

[58]*Temps et autrui.*

PART IV

P art III began with suffering as the event whereby the existent manages to accomplish all its solitude—that is, all the intensity of its tie with itself, all the finality of its identity—and at the same time it is that whereby the subject finds itself in relationship with the event that it does not assume, which is absolutely other, and in regard to which it is a pure passivity and no longer able to be able. This future of death determines the future for us, the future insofar as it is not present. It determines what in the future contrasts strongly with all anticipation, projection, and élan. Starting from such a notion of the future to understand time, one never again meets with time as a "moving image of eternity."[59]

When one deprives the present of all anticipation, the future loses all co-naturalness with it. The future is not buried in the bowels of a preexistent eternity, where we would come to lay hold of it. It is absolutely other and new. And it is thus that one can understand the very reality of time, the absolute impossibility of finding in the present the equivalent of the future, the lack of any hold upon the future.

To be sure, the Bergsonian conception of freedom through duration tends toward the same end. But it preserves for the present a power over the future: duration is creation. To criticize this deathless philosophy it is not enough to situate it within the whole drift of modern philosophy, which makes creation the principal attribute of the creature. It is a matter of showing that creation itself presupposes an opening onto a mystery. The subject's identity

[59]Plato, *Timaeus*, 37; also see p. 129 below.

by itself is incapable of yielding this. To uphold this thesis I have insisted upon the anonymous and irremissible existing that constitutes an entire universe, and upon the hypostasis that ends in the mastery of an existent over existing, but which by the same token is shut up within the finality of the identity that its spatial transcendence does not undo. It is not a matter of contesting the fact of anticipation, to which the Bergsonian descriptions of duration have accustomed us. It is a matter of showing their ontological conditions, which are the feat rather than the work[60] of a subject in relation with mystery, which is, so to say, the very dimension that is opened to a subject shut up in itself. This is precisely the reason why the work of time is profound. It is not simply a renewal through creation, which remains attached to the present, giving the creature but the sadness of Pygmalion. More than the renewal of our moods and qualities, time is essentially a new birth.

POWER AND RELATIONSHIP WITH THE OTHER

The strangeness of the future of death does not leave the subject any initiative. There is an abyss between the present and death, between the ego and the alterity of mystery. It is not the fact that death cuts existence short, that it is end and nothingness, but the fact that the ego is absolutely without initiative in the face of it. Vanquishing death is not a problem of eternal life. Vanquishing death is to maintain, with the alterity of the event, a relationship that must still be personal.

What, then, is this personal relationship other than the subject's power over the world, meanwhile protecting its personality? How can the subject be given a definition that somehow lies in its passivity? Is there another mastery in

[60]*le fait plutôt que l'oeuvre.*

the human other than the virility of grasping the possible, the *power to be able* [*"pouvoir de pouvoir"*]? If we find it, it is in it, in this relation that very place of time will consist. I already said in Part III that this relation is the relationship with the Other.

But a solution does not consist in repeating the terms of the problem. It is a matter of specifying what this relationship with the Other can be. Someone has objected to me that in my relationship with the Other it is not only the Other's future that I encounter, that the other as existent already has a past for me and, consequently, does not have a privilege over the future. This objection will allow me to approach the main part of my exposition here. I do not define the other by the future, but the future by the other, for the very future of death consists in its total alterity. But my main response will consist in saying that the relationship with the other, taken at the level of our civilization, is a complication of our original relationship; it is in no way a contingent complication, but one itself founded upon the inner dialectic of the relationship with the Other. I cannot develop this here.[61] I will simply say that this dialectic appears when one pushes further all the implications of hypostasis that have thus far been treated very schematically, and in particular when one shows, next to the transcendence toward the world, the transcendence of expression that founds the contemporaneousness of civilization and the mutuality of every relationship. But this transcendence of expression itself presupposes the future of alterity, to which I limit myself here.

If the relationship with the other involves more than relationships with mystery, it is because one has accosted the other in everyday life where the solitude and fundamental alterity of the other are already veiled by decency. One is

[61]For these developments, see the section entitled "Intentions" in *Existence and Existents*, pp. 37–45; and the section entitled "The Truth of the Will" in *Totality and Infinity*, pp. 240–47.

for the other what the other is for oneself; there is no exceptional place for the subject. The other is known through
sympathy, as another (my)self, as the alter ego.[62] In Blanchot's novel *Aminadab,* this situation is pushed to the absurd. Between the persons circulating in the strange house
where the action takes place, where there is no work to
pursue, where they only abide—that is, exist—this social
relationship becomes total reciprocity. These beings are not
interchangeable but reciprocal, or rather they are interchangeable because they are reciprocal. And then the relationship with the other becomes impossible.

But already, in the very heart of the relationship with the
other that characterizes our social life, alterity appears as a
nonreciprocal relationship—that is, as contrasting strongly
with contemporaneousness. The Other as Other is not only
an alter ego: the Other is what I myself am not.[63] The Other
is this, not because of the Other's character, or physi-
ognomy, or psychology, but because of the Other's very alterity. The Other is, for example, the weak, the poor, "the
widow and the orphan,"[64] whereas I am the rich or the
powerful. It can be said that intersubjective space is not

[62]It is at the level of the "decency" of "everyday life" then, that Levinas
finds a place for the sympathy and pairing that he has rejected as ultimately constitutive of the inter-subjective relationship (see notes 50 and
51, above).

[63]For Levinas this formulation does not necessarily lead to the conclusion of the German Idealists—namely, that alterity is only encountered
through *negation.* Philosophers can perhaps hardly be reminded too often
of this difference. For Levinas the alterity encountered through negativity
is merely a relative, not an absolute, alterity. To grasp alterity *outside* even
negativity, and thus in a truly positive "sense," is perhaps the essence of
Levinas' entire effort. See, in particular, the section entitled "Transcendence is Not Negativity" in *Totality and Infinity,* pp. 40–42; and the Preface,
above (p. 32).

[64]The Hebrew Bible contains many references to the orphan and the
widow jointly: Exodus 22:21; Deuteronomy 10:18, 24:17, 24:19, 24:20,
24:21, 26:12, 27:19; Isaiah 1:17, 9:16, 10:2; Jeremiah 7:6, 22:3; Ezekiel 22:7;
Zechariah 7:10; Malachi 3:5; Psalms 68:6, 109:9, 146:9; Lamentations 5:3.
Relevant to Levinas' emphasis on the alterity of the other, in all these instances (except Isaiah, and at 68:6 in Psalms where the "solitary" is men-

symmetrical.[65] The exteriority of the other is not simply due to the space that separates what remains identical through the concept, nor is it due to any difference the concept would manifest through spatial exteriority. The relationship with alterity is neither spatial nor conceptual. Durkheim has misunderstood the specificity of the other when he asks in what Other rather than myself is the object of a virtuous action.[66] Does not the essential difference between charity and justice come from the preference of charity for the other, even when, from the point of view of justice, no preference is any longer possible?[67]

Eros[68]

In civilized life there are traces of this relationship with the other that one must investigate in its original form.

[65] See the section entitled "The Asymmetry of the Interpersonal" in Totality and Infinity, pp. 215-16, also p. 251 and passim.

[66] According to Durkheim, "morality is the product of the collective" and not the result of the face-to-face encounter. See "The Determination of Moral Facts" and "Replies to Objections" in Emile Durkheim, Sociology and Philosophy, translated by D. Pocock (New York: MacMillan Publishing Co., 1974), pp. 35-79.

[67] Although, inasmuch as our culture is predominately Christian, one might see here an allusion only to the alleged opposition between "Christian mercy" and "Jewish justice," in addition to being an internal Christian opposition (often enough, it is true, expressed in terms of a Christian vision of Judaism), the allusion here is certainly also to an ancient and properly internal Jewish opposition—namely, that between God's chesed, kindness, and God's gevurah, justice. To be sure, this opposition is equally a secular, moral opposition.

[68] For a fuller development of the analysis of eros and fecundity (the topic of the next section), see section 4, "Beyond the Face," of Totality and Infinity, pp. 254-85. Also see "Phenomenology of the Face and Carnal Intimacy" by A. Lingis in his book, Libido: The French Existential Theories (Bloomington: Indiana University Press, 1985), pp. 58-73; and "The Fecundity of the Caress" by L. Irigaray, in Face to Face with Levinas, edited by R. Cohen (Albany: State University of New York Press, 1986), pp. 231-56.

tioned; and, one should add, in James 1:27, where the orphan and the widow are mentioned together), the stranger is always also mentioned in conjunction with the orphan and the widow.

Does a situation exist where the alterity of the other appears in its purity? Does a situation exist where the other would not have alterity only as the reverse side of its identity, would not comply only with the Platonic law of participation where every term contains a sameness and through this sameness contains the Other? Is there not a situation where alterity would be borne by a being in a positive sense, as essence? What is the alterity that does not purely and simply enter into the opposition of two species of the same genus? I think the absolutely contrary contrary [*le contraire absolutement contraire*], whose contrariety is in no way affected by the relationship that can be established between it and its correlative, the contrariety that permits its terms to remain absolutely other, is the *feminine.*[69]

Sex is not some specific difference. It is situated beside the logical division into genera and species. This division certainly never manages to reunite an empirical content. But it is not in this sense that it does not permit one to account for the difference between the sexes. The difference between the sexes is a formal structure, but one that carves up reality in another sense and conditions the very possibility of reality as multiple, against the unity of being proclaimed by Parmenides.

Neither is the difference between the sexes a contradiction. The contradiction of being and nothingness leads from one to the other, leaving no room for distance. Noth-

[69]This sentence and some of those that follow were cited by Simone de Beauvoir in 1949 in *The Second Sex* (translated by H. Parshley [New York: Bantam Books, Inc., 1970], p. xvi, n. 3) to condemn Levinas for sexism.

De Beauvoir takes Levinas to task for allegedly assigning a secondary, derivative status to women: subject (he) as absolute, woman as other. The issue is important but certainly not as simple as de Beauvoir, in this instance, makes it out to be, because for Levinas the other has a priority over the subject. For a more sympathetic treatment of Levinas' thought on this issue, see C. Chalier, *Figures du féminin* (Paris: La nuit surveillée, 1982).

For Levinas' most recent thoughts on this issue, with regard to *Time and the Other*, see "Love and Filiation" in Levinas, *Ethics and Infinity*, translated by R. Cohen (Pittsburgh: Duquesne University Press, 1985), pp. 65–72.

ingness converts into being, which has led us to the notion of the "there is." The negation of being occurs at the level of the anonymous existing of being in general.

Neither is the difference between the sexes the duality of two complementary terms, for two complementary terms presuppose a preexisting whole. To say that sexual duality presupposes a whole is to posit love beforehand as fusion.[70] The pathos of love, however, consists in an insurmountable duality of beings. It is a relationship with what always slips away. The relationship does not *ipso facto* neutralize alterity but preserves it. The pathos of voluptuousness lies in the fact of being two. The other as other is not here an object that becomes ours or becomes us; to the contrary, it withdraws into its mystery. Neither does this mystery of the feminine—the feminine: essentially other—refer to any romantic notions of the mysterious, unknown, or misunderstood woman. Let it be understood that if, in order to uphold the thesis of the exceptional position of the feminine in the economy of being, I willingly refer to the great themes of Goethe or Dante, to Beatrice and the *ewig Weibliches*, to the cult of the *Woman* in chivalry and in modern society (which is certainly not explained solely by the necessity of lending a strong arm to the weaker sex)—if, more precisely, I think of the admirably bold pages of Léon Bloy in his *Letters to his Fiancée*,[71] I do not want to ignore the legitimate claims of the feminism that presupposes all the acquired attainments of civilization. I simply want to say that this mystery must not be understood in the ethereal sense of a certain literature; that in the most brutal materiality, in the most shameless or the most prosaic appearance of the feminine, neither her mystery nor her modesty are abolished. Profanation is not a negation of mystery, but one of the possible relationships with it.

This is Aristophanes' position in Plato's *Symposium*.

Lettres à sa Fiancée (Paris: Stock, 1922); English translation (New York: Sheed and Ward, 1937). Léon Bloy (1846–1917) was a prolific French Catholic writer with a strong Jansenist bent.

What matters to me in this notion of the feminine is not merely the unknowable, but a mode of being that consists in slipping away from the light. The feminine in existence is an event different from that of spatial transcendence or of expression that go toward light. It is a flight before light. Hiding is the way of existing of the feminine, and this fact of hiding is precisely modesty. So this feminine alterity does not consist in the object's simple exteriority. Neither is it made up of an opposition of wills. The Other is not a being we encounter that menaces us or wants to lay hold of us. The feat of being refractory to our power is not a power greater than ours. Alterity makes for all its power. Its mystery constitutes its alterity. A fundamental comment: I do not initially posit the Other as freedom, a characteristic in which the failure of communication is inscribed in advance. For with a freedom there can be no other relationship than that of submission or enslavement. In both cases, one of the two freedoms is annihilated. The relationship between master and slave can be grasped at the level of struggle, but then it becomes reciprocal. Hegel has shown precisely how the master becomes slave of the slave and the slave becomes master of the master.[72]

In positing the Other's alterity as mystery, itself defined by modesty, I do not posit it as a freedom identical to and at grips with mine; I do not posit another existent in front of me, I posit alterity. Just as with death, I am not concerned with an existent, but with the event of alterity, with alienation. The other is not initially characterized as freedom, from which alterity would then be deduced; the other

[72]Surely, in addition to Hegel, Levinas has Sartre's philosophy of freedom in mind. *Being and Nothingness* was published only five years earlier than *Time and the Other* (although Levinas, a German captive for the duration of W.W. II, had not yet read it in 1946, by his own admission [see Jean Wahl, *A Short History of Existentialism*, translated by F. Williams and S. Maron (New York: Philosophical Library, 1949)], p. 51).

For some recent critical remarks by Levinas on the early Sartre, see Richard Kearney's "Dialogue with Emmanuel Levinas," in *Face to Face with Levinas*, edited by R. Cohen (Albany: State University of New York Press, 1986), pp. 16–17.

bears alterity as an essence. And this is why I have sought this alterity in the absolutely original relationship of eros, a relationship that is impossible to translate into powers and must not be so translated, if one does not want to distort the meaning of the situation.

I am thus describing a category that falls neither into the being-nothingness opposition, nor into the notion of the existent. It is an event in existing different from the hypostasis by which an existent arises. The existent is accomplished in the "subjective" and in "consciousness"; alterity is accomplished in the feminine. This term is on the same level as, but in meaning opposed to, consciousness. The feminine is not accomplished as a *being* [*étant*] in a transcendence toward light, but in modesty.

The movement here is thus inverse. The transcendence of the feminine consists in withdrawing elsewhere, which is a movement opposed to the movement of consciousness. But this does not make it unconscious or subconscious, and I see no other possibility than to call it mystery.

Even when by positing the Other as freedom, by thinking of the Other in terms of light, I am obliged to admit the failure of communication, I have merely admitted the failure of the movement that tends to grasp or to possess a freedom. It is only by showing in what way eros differs from possession and power that I can acknowledge a communication in eros. It is neither a struggle, nor a fusion, nor a knowledge. One must recognize its exceptional place among relationships. It is a relationship with alterity, with mystery—that is to say, with the future, with what (in a world where there is everything) is never there, with what cannot be there when everything is there—not with a being that is not there, but with the very dimension of alterity. There where all possibles are impossible, where one can no longer be able, the subject is still a subject through eros. Love is not a possibility, is not due to our initiative, is without reason; it invades and wounds us, and nevertheless the *I* survives in it.

A phenomenology of voluptuousness, which I am only going to touch upon here—voluptuousness is not a pleasure like others, because it is not solitary like eating or drinking—seems to confirm my views on the exceptional role and place of the feminine, and on the absence of any fusion in the erotic.

The caress is a mode of the subject's being, where the subject who is in contact with another goes beyond this contact. Contact as sensation is part of the world of light. But what is caressed is not touched, properly speaking. It is not the softness or warmth of the hand given in contact that the caress seeks. The seeking of the caress constitutes its essence by the fact that the caress does not know what it seeks. This "not knowing," this fundamental disorder, is the essential. It is like a game with something slipping away, a game absolutely without project or plan, not with what can become ours or us, but with something other, always other, always inaccessible, and always still to come [*à venir*]. The caress is the anticipation of this pure future [*avenir*],[73] without content. It is made up of this increase of hunger, of ever richer promises, opening new perspectives onto the ungraspable. It feeds on countless hungers.

This intentionality of the voluptuous—the sole intentionality of the future itself, and not an expectation of some future fact—has always been misunderstood by philosophical analysis. Freud himself says little more about the libido than that it searches for pleasure, taking pleasure as a simple content, starting with which one begins an analysis but

[73]*Venir* is a verb meaning "to come" or—especially in the construction *à venir*—"about to come"; *avenir* is a noun meaning "future." These latter two terms sound exactly the same in French. Levinas is emphasizing the essential connection between their meanings: the future is what is always about to come—that is, what is always about to come into the present but has not yet done so and never will (lest it be present rather than future).

which itself one does not analyze. Freud does not search for the significance of this pleasure in the general economy of being. My thesis, which consists in affirming voluptuousness as the very event of the future, the future purified of all content, the very mystery of the future, seeks to account for its exceptional place.

Can this relationship with the other through Eros be characterized as a failure? Once again, the answer is yes, if one adopts the terminology of current descriptions, if one wants to characterize the erotic by "grasping," "possessing," or "knowing." But there is nothing of all this, or the failure of all this, in eros. If one could possess, grasp, and know the other, it would not be other. Possessing, knowing, and grasping are synonyms of power.

Furthermore, the relationship with the other is generally sought out as a fusion. I have precisely wanted to contest the idea that the relationship with the other is fusion. The relationship with the Other is the absence of the other; not absence pure and simple, not the absence of pure nothingness, but absence in a horizon of the future, an absence that is time. This is the horizon where a personal life can be constituted in the heart of the transcendent event, what I called above the "victory over death." I must say a few words about it in concluding.

FECUNDITY[74]

I am going to return to the consideration that led me from the alterity of death to the alterity of the feminine. Before a pure event, a pure future, which is death, where the ego can in no way be able—that is, can no longer be an ego—I seek a situation where nonetheless it is possible for it to remain an ego, and I have called this situation "victory over

[74]See note 68, above.

death." Once again, this situation cannot be qualified as power. How, in the alterity of a you, can I remain I, without being absorbed or losing myself in that you? How can the ego that I am remain myself in a you, without being none-theless the ego that I am in my present—that is to say, an ego that inevitably returns to itself? How can the ego be-come other to itself? This can happen only in one way: through paternity.

Paternity is the relationship with a stranger who, entirely while being Other, is myself, the relationship of the ego with a myself who is nonetheless a stranger to me. The son, in effect, is not simply my work, like a poem or an arti-fact, neither is he my property. Neither the categories of power nor those of having can indicate the relationship with the child. Neither the notion of cause nor the notion of ownership permit one to grasp the fact of fecundity. I do not *have* my child; I *am* in some way my child. But the words "I am" here have a significance different from an Ele-atic or Platonic significance. There is a multiplicity and a transcendence in this verb "to exist," a transcendence that is lacking in even the boldest existentialist analyses. Then again, the son is not any event whatsoever that happens to me—for example, my sadness, my ordeal, or my suffering. The son is an ego, a person. Lastly, the alterity of the son is not that of an alter ego. Paternity is not a sympathy through which I can put myself in the son's place. It is through my being, not through sympathy, that I am my son. The return of the ego to itself that begins with hypostasis is thus not without remission, thanks to the perspective of the future opened by eros. Instead of obtaining this remission through the impossible dissolution of hypostasis, one ac-complishes it through the son. It is thus not according to the category of cause, but according to the category of the father that freedom comes about and time is accomplished.

Bergson's notion of *élan vital*, which merges artistic crea-tion and generation in the same movement—what I call "fecundity"—does not take account of death, but above all it tends toward an impersonal pantheism, in the sense that it does not sufficiently note the crispation and isolation of subjectivity, which is the ineluctable moment of my dialectic. Paternity is not simply the renewal of the father in the son and the father's merger with him, it is also the father's exteriority in relation to the son, a pluralist existing. The fecundity of the ego must be appreciated at its correct ontological value, which until now has never been done. The fact that it is a biological—and psychological—category in no way neutralizes the paradox of its significance.

I began with the notions of death and the feminine, and have ended with that of the son. I have not proceeded in a phenomenological way. The continuity of development is that of a dialectic starting with the identity of hypostasis, the enchainment of the ego to the self, moving toward the maintenance of this identity, toward the maintenance of the existent, but in a liberation of the ego with regard to self. The concrete situations that have been analyzed represent the accomplishment of this dialectic. Many intermediaries have been skipped. The unity of these situations—death, sexuality, paternity—until now appeared only in relation to the notion of power that they exclude.

This was my main goal. I have been bent on emphasizing that alterity is not purely and simply the existence of another freedom next to mine. I have a power over such a freedom where it is absolutely foreign to me, without relation to me. The coexistence of several freedoms is a multiplicity that leaves the unity of each intact, or else this multiplicity unites into a general will. Sexuality, paternity, and death introduce a duality into existence, a duality that concerns the very existing of each subject. Existing itself becomes double. The Eleatic notion of being is overcome. Time constitutes not the fallen form of being, but its very event. The Eleatic notion of being dominates Plato's philosophy, where multiplicity was subordinated to the one, and where the role of the feminine was thought within the categories of passivity and activity, and was reduced to matter. Plato did not grasp the feminine in its specifically erotic notion. In his philosophy of love he left to the feminine no other role than that of furnishing an example of the Idea, which alone can be the object of love. The whole particularity of the relationship of one to another goes unnoticed. Plato constructs a Republic that must imitate the world of Ideas; he makes a philosophy of a world of light, a world without time. Beginning with Plato, the social ideal will be sought for in an ideal of fusion. It will be thought that, in its relationship with the other, the subject tends to be identified with the other, by being swallowed up in a collective representation,[75] a common ideal. It is the collectivity that says "we," that, turned toward the intelligible sun, toward the truth, feels the other at its side and not in front of itself. This collectivity necessarily establishes itself around a third term, which serves as an intermediary. *Miteinandersein*, too, remains the collectivity of the "with," and is revealed in its authentic form around the truth. It is a collectivity around something common. Just as in all the philosophies of communion, sociality in Heidegger is found in the subject alone; and it is in terms of solitude that the analysis of *Dasein* in its authentic form is pursued.

Against this collectivity of the side-by-side, I have tried to oppose the "I-you" collectivity,[76] taking this not in Buber's sense, where reciprocity remains the tie between two sepa-

[75]The term "collective representation" was used by the *l'année sociologique* group of anthropologists, including Durkheim, Mauss, and Levy-Bruhl. See, again, Lucian Levy-Bruhl, *How Natives Think* (Princeton University Press, 1985), translated by L. Clare; especially the Introduction and part 1, chapter 1, "Collective Representation in Primitives' Perceptions and the Mystical Character of Such," pp. 13–76.

[76]Of course Sartre also rejects the collectivity of the side-by-side in the name of the "I-you" (Sartre, *Being and Nothingness*, part 3, chapter 1). But, as we have seen, for Levinas, Sartre's criticism is inadequate because the "I-you" it proposes remains an antagonistic relationship of two freedoms, a failure of communication.

rated freedoms, and the ineluctable character of isolated subjectivity is underestimated.[77] I have tried to find the temporal transcendence of the present toward the mystery of the future. This is not a participation in a third term, whether this term be a person, a truth, a work, or a profession. It is a collectivity that is not a communion. It is the face-to-face without intermediary, and is furnished for us in the eros where, in the other's proximity, distance is integrally maintained, and whose pathos is made of both this proximity and this duality.

What one presents as the failure of communication in love precisely constitutes the positivity of the relationship; this absence of the other is precisely its presence as other.

Set against the cosmos that is Plato's world, is the world of the spirit [l'esprit] where the implications of eros are not reduced to the logic of genus, and where the ego takes the place of the same and the Other takes the place of the other.

---

[77]For a deeper understanding of Levinas' reading of Buber, see (among other articles) Levinas, "Martin Buber and the Theory of Knowledge," in The Philosophy of Martin Buber, edited by P. Schillp and M. Friedman (La Salle, Illinois: Open Court, 1967), pp. 133–50; and their subsequent correspondence in "Dialogue avec Martin Buber," in Levinas, Noms Propre (Montpellier: Fata Morgana, 1976), pp. 51–55.

Other Essays

Diachrony and Representation
(1982)

KNOWLEDGE AND PRESENCE

The sphere of intelligibility—the reasonable—in which everyday life as well as the tradition of our philosophic and scientific thought maintains itself, is characterized by vision. The structure of a *seeing* having the *seen* for its object or theme—the so-called intentional structure—is found in all the modes of sensibility having access to things. It is found in the *intellectual* accession to the state-of-things or to the relationships between things. But apparently it is also found in the company human beings keep among themselves, between beings who speak to one another, and of whom it is said that they "see one another." Thus the priority of knowledge is announced, where all that we call thought, intelligence, mind, or simply psychism, ties together.

Thought, intelligence, mind, and psychism would be *conscious*, or on the threshold of consciousness. Human consciousness would be a perfect modality: the consciousness of an ego *identical* in its *I think*, aiming at and embracing, or perceiving, all alterity under its thematizing gaze. This aiming of thought is called intentionality. This is a remarkable word, which first indicates the thematization of a *seeing* and, in some way, the contemplative character of psychism, its being-at-a-distance from what is contemplated, which one easily takes for a model of dis-interestedness. But intentionality also indicates an aspiration,

finality, and desire, a moment of egoism or egotism and, in
any case, "egology." This is a moment that certainly ani-
mates what are called "pulsions," regardless of how little
one distinguishes them from a purely kinetic phenomenon
in the physicist's object. In this sense, consciousness, of
which the unconscious is itself a deficient mode, remains
truly the dominant characteristic of our interpretation of
the mind [esprit]. The other, "intentionally" aimed at, invested, and assembled by the apperception of the I think,
comes—through thought as thought, through the noema—to
fulfill, fill, or satisfy the aim, desire or aspiration of the I
think or its noesis. The other is thus present to the ego. And
this "being-present," or this presence of the "I think" to the
ego, is equivalent to being.

Presence or being is also a temporal modality. But it then
concretely signifies an ex-position of the other to the ego,
and thus signifies precisely an offering of itself, a giving of itself, a Gegebenheit. It is a donation of alterity within presence, not only in the metaphorical sense of the term, but as
a donation signifying within a concrete horizon of a taking
already referred to a "taking in hand." This essential "now"
[main-tenance], if one can say so, the presence of the
present, as temporality, is the promise of a graspable, a
solid. It is what is probably the very promotion of the thing,
the "something," of the configuration of a being [étant] in
being [être], in presence. And this prototypical lineament of
the knowledge of things is the prerequisite of the abstrac-
tions of the idealized knowledge of understanding, as the
phenomenology of the Husserlian Crisis—but already, in
principle, of the Logical Investigations—has taught us.

The technical possibilities of knowledge and seeing,
then, contrast less vividly with the alleged theoretical purity and the alleged contemplative serenity of the truth and
the time of pure presence and pure re-presentation. These
possibilities and technical temptations are their horizon.
They are much less out of tune with the alleged dis-inter-

estedness of theory than is thought by the critics of the in-
dustrial modernity denounced as deviation and
corruption. Seeing or knowing, and taking in hand, are
tied together in the structure of intentionality. It remains
the intrigue of a thought that recognizes itself in consciousness: the "now" [*main-tainance*] of the present emphasizes
immanence as the very excellence of this thought.

But, then, the intelligibility and intelligence situated in
thought understood as vision and knowledge, interpreted
starting from intentionality, consist in privileging, in the
very temporality of thought, the present in relation to the
past and future. To comprehend the alteration of presence
in the past and future would be a matter of reducing and
bringing back the past and future to presence—that is, re-
presenting them. And, seemingly, it would be a matter of
understanding all alterity, which is brought together, welcomed, and synchronized in the presence at the interior of
the *I think*, and which then is assumed in the identity of the
Ego—it is a matter of understanding this alterity assumed
by the thought of the identical—as *its own* and, then still, of
leading its *other* back to the *same.* The other is made the
property of the ego in the knowledge that assures the mar-
vel of immanence. Intentionality is the aimed at, and in the
thematization of being—that is, in presence—is a return to
self as much as an escape from self.

In thought understood as vision, knowledge, and intentionality, intelligibility thus signifies the reduction of the
other [*Autre*] to the Same, synchrony as *being* in its egological gathering. The *known* expresses the unity of the transcendental apperception of the *cogito,* or the Kantian *I
think,* the egology of presence affirmed from Descartes to
Husserl, and up to Heidegger where, in paragraph 9 of *Being and Time, Dasein*'s "toward-being" [*à-être*] is the source
of *Jemeinigkeit* and thus of the Ego.

Does not the "seeing one another" between humans—
that is to say, clearly, language—revert, in its turn, to a see-

ing, and thus to this egological significance of intentionality, the egology of synthesis, the gathering of all alterity into presence, and the synchrony of representation? Language is usually understood thus.

To be sure, in speaking, knowledge and seeing have recourse to signs and are communicated in verbal signs to the Other—which would overflow the pure egological gathering of the signified into thematized presence. And, to be sure, the problem remains as to the motive for this communication. Why do we give an account to the other? Because we have something to say. But why is this known or represented something said? And even so the recourse to signs does not necessarily presuppose this communication. It can be justified by the necessity the ego finds—in its solitary synthesis of apperception—of giving signs to itself, before speaking to anyone else. In its egological work of gathering the diverse into presence or into representation, it can, beyond immediate presence, search for the presence of what is already past or of what has not yet come about, and then recall them, foresee them, or name them, by signs. One can thus even write for oneself. That one cannot have thought without language, without recourse to verbal signs, would not then attest to any definitive rupture in the egological order of presence. It would only signify the necessity of interior discourse. Finite thought is split in order to interrogate and answer itself, but the thread is retied. Thought reflects on itself in interrupting its continuity of synthetic apperception, but still proceeds from the same "I think" or returns to it. It can even, in this gathering, pass from one term to another term apparently exclusive of the first, but which, owing to its very exclusion, would be announced and already recuperated. The dialectic that tears the ego apart ends by a synthesis and system whereby the tear is no longer seen. Dialectic is not a dialogue with the Other, or at least it remains a "dialogue of the soul with itself, proceeding by questions and answers." Plato precisely defined thought thus. According to the traditional interpretation of discourse that goes back to this definition, the mind in speaking its thought remains no less one and unique, the same in presence, a synchrony despite its coming-and-going where the ego could be opposed to itself.

Unity and presence are maintained in the empirical reality of inter-human speaking. For each of the interlocutors, speaking would consist in entering *within* the thought of the other, in holding to it. This coincidence is Reason and interiority. Here the thinking subjects are obscure multiple points, empirically antagonistic, in whom illumination occurs when they see each other, speak to each other, and coincide. The exchange of ideas will produce presence or representation in the unity of an utterance or an account naming or displaying a knowledge. It would fit within a single consciousness, in a *cogito* that remains Reason: universal Reason and egological interiority.

Language can pass for interior discourse and can always be attributed to the gathering of alterity into the unity of presence by the *ego* of the intentional *I think*. Even if the Other enters into this language—which is indeed possible—reference to the egological work of representation is not interrupted by this entry. It would not be interrupted even when presence, beyond the re-presentation accomplished in memory and imagination, is assured by the investigations of the historian and the futurologist, or when, in a cultivated humanity, writing gathers the past and future into the presence of a book—something between bindings—or the presence of a library united on bookshelves. This is the gathering of a history into the presence of a thing, the gathering of the being of a being into a being [*l'être de l'étant dans un étant*]! It is the key moment of re-presentation and vision as the essence of thought! And it is this despite all the time that the reading of a book can take, where this gathering, or this texture of presence, returns to duration. And it is this, above all, despite the past which had neither been present nor re-presented by anyone—the immemorial or an-archic past—and despite the inspired future, which no one anticipates. Such a past and future begin to signify time starting from the hermeneutic of the "verses" of a text, without prior chronological reference to the metaphor of flux or to the still spatial images of the "hither" and "beyond."

Has time *thus* valorized its incompressible intrigue? It has already been valorized in certain chiaroscuros of the phenomenology of time whose masterful example Husserl has already given us, where the intentionality of re-tention and pro-tention would have, on the one hand, reduced the time of consciousness understood as the consciousness of time to the re-presentation of the living present—that is, still as the re-presentation of presence: "the being of beings," which it signifies—but where, on the other hand, the *retaining* of re-tension differs from the protending of pro-tention only through the comprehension of time already given and pre-supposed in this very constitution—that is, as a time slipping by like a flux. This metaphor of "flux" lives off a temporality borrowed from the *being* that is a liquid whose particles are in movement, a movement already accomplishing itself in time.

It is necessary, then, to ask if even the discourse that is called interior, which thus remains egological and measures up to re-presentation, despite its scission into questions and answers addressed by the ego to itself, where the association of several individuals is possible on condition that "each enters into the thought of the others," one must ask if this very discourse, despite its allegedly interior scissions, does not already rest on a prior sociality with the Other where the interlocutors are distinct. It is necessary to ask if this forgotten but effective sociality is not nonetheless presupposed by the rupture, however provisional, between self and self, for the interior dialogue to still deserve the name dialogue. This sociality is irreducible to the immanence of representation, is other than the sociality that would be reduced to the knowledge one can acquire about the Other as a known object, and would already support the immanence of an ego having an experience of world. Does not the interior dialogue presuppose, beyond the *representation* of the Other, a relationship to the other person as other, and not at first a relationship to the *other* already apperceived as the *same* through a reason that is universal from the start?

The moment has come to ask if this entry of each into the representation of the others, if this agreement between thoughts in the synchrony of the given, is the unique, original, and ultimate rationality of thought and discourse? And one must ask if this gathering of time into presence by intentionality, and thus if the reduction of time to the essance of being, its reducibility to presence and representation, is the primordial intrigue of time? And one must ask if the manifestation of presence, if appearing, is equivalent to rationality? Is language only reasonable in its *said [dit]*, in its indicative propositions which are all at least latent, in the theoretical aspect of affirmed or virtual judgments, in pure communications of information? Is language only reasonable in its *said*, in all that can be written? Is it not reasonable in the sociality of *saying [dire]*, in responsibility with regard to the Other who commands the questions and answers of the saying, and through the "nonpresence" or the "appresentation" of the interlocutor who thus contrasts strongly with the presence of things according to the underlying simultaneity of the given universe? From the ego to this interlocutor there is a temporality other than the one that allows itself to be assembled into the presence of the *said* and the *written*, a temporality that is concrete in this "from-me-to-the-other," but which at once congeals into the abstraction of the synchronous in the synthesis of the "I think" that grasps it thematically.

Is it necessary to attribute an unconditional priority in

the signification of meaning to this thematizing and theoretical grasp and to the order that is its *noematic* correlative,
the order of presence, being as being, and objectivity? Is it
there that meaning arises? Should not knowledge interrogate itself about itself and its justification? Does not this
justification—in its semantic context of rightness and
justice—thus go back to the responsibility for the Other—
that is, to the proximity of the neighbor—as to the very domain of intelligibility or original rationality where, on this
side of every theoretical explanation, in the human, the being that until then is justified in its natural unfolding as being, and as giving itself out to be the beginning of all
rationalization, is brusquely put into question in me and
finds a pre-initial rightness?

I have tried to show elsewhere[1] that the judgments of
true knowledge and thematic thought are summoned—or
invented—starting from or apropos of certain exigencies
that depend on the ethical significance of the Other, inscribed in his face—imperatives in the face of the other who
is incomparable to me and is unique, certain exigencies that
make justice concrete. That justice is thus found to be the
source of the objectivity of logical judgment, and that it has
to support the entire level of theoretical thought, does not
amount to denouncing rationality or the structure of intentional thought, or the synchronization of the diverse that it
involves, or the thematization of being by synthetic
thought, or the problematic of ontology. But I also think
that the latter constitute the rationality of an already derived order, that responsibility for the Other signifies an
original and concrete temporality, and that the universal-
ization of presence presupposes it. I also think that the sociality where responsibility is made concrete in justice calls
for and founds the objectivity of theoretical language,
which "gathers" the diachrony of time into presence and

[1]Levinas: See my *Otherwise than Being or Beyond Essence*, pp. 160–61 and
42–43.

representation through accounts and histories, and—*up to a certain point*—understands reason—in view of justice itself—by *comparing* "incomparable and unique" persons in a knowing thought, comparing them as *beings*—that is, as individuals of a genus. I also think that institutions, courts, and thus the State, must concretely appear in this derived order of rationality.

But if it is not a matter, starting from this analysis, of denouncing the intentional structure of thought as alienation, by showing its development from out of the "proximity of the neighbor" and "responsibility for the Other," it is nevertheless important to lay stress on this development. The State, institutions, and even the courts that they support, reveal themselves essentially to an eventually inhuman but characteristic determinism—politics. Hence it is important to be able to check this determinism in going back to its motivation in justice and a foundational inter-humanity. We have just taken some steps in this direction.

ALTERITY AND DIACHRONY

I begin by asking if, to an ego, the alterity of the other person first signifies a logical alterity. The latter marks each part in a *whole* vis-à-vis the others, where, in a purely formal way, one, this one, is other to that one, and that one is, by the same token, other to this one. Between the persons included in this reciprocity, language would be only a reciprocal exchange of information or anecdotes, intentionally aimed at and gathered together in the enunciation of each partner. Or if, as I am inclined to think, the alterity of the other person to an ego is first—and I dare to say, is "positively"—the face of the other person obligating the ego, which, from the first—without deliberation—is responsive to the Other. *From the first*, that is, the ego answers "gratuitously," without worrying about reciprocity. This is the gratuitousness of the *for-the-other*, the response of responsibility that already lies dormant in a salutation, in the *hello*, in the *goodbye*. Such a language is anterior to the enunciation of propositions communicating information and accounts. The *for-the-other* responsive to the neighbor, in the proximity of the neighbor, is a responsibility that signifies—or commands—precisely the face in its alterity and its ineffaceable and unassumable authority of *facing up*. (Whom does one face? Whence the authority? Questions not to lose sight of!) But the *for-the-other* in the approach of the face—a for-the-other older than *consciousness of. . .* — precedes all *grasping* in its obedience, and remains prior to the intentionality of the ego-subject in its being-in-the-world, which presents itself and gives itself a synthesized and synchronous world. The *for-the-other* dawns in the ego as a commandment understood by the ego in its very obedience, as if obedience were its very accession to hearing the prescription, as if the ego obeyed before having understood, and as if the intrigue of alterity were knotted prior to knowledge.

But here the simplicity of this primary obedience is upset by the third person emerging next to the other; the third person is himself also a neighbor, and the responsibility of the ego also devolves onto him. Here, starting from this third person, is the proximity of a human plurality. Who, in this plurality, comes first? Here is the hour and birthplace of the question: a demand for justice! Here is the obligation to compare unique and incomparable others; here is the hour of *knowledge* and, then, of the objectivity beyond or on the hither side of the nudity of the face; here is the hour of consciousness and intentionality. Objectivity issues from justice and is founded on justice, and is thus exerted by the *for-the-other*, which, in the alterity of the face, commands the ego. Here is the call to re-presentation that does not cease to cover the nudity of the face and to give it a content and countenance in a world. The objectivity of justice—which is rigorous in this aspect—obscures the alterity of the face that originally signifies, or commands, outside the context of the world, and does not cease, in its enigma or ambiguity, to tear itself away from and to make exception to the plastic forms of the presence and objectivity that it nonetheless calls forth even while it appeals to justice.

The exteriority of the face is extra-ordinary. It is extra-ordinary for order is justice. It is extra-ordinary or absolute in the etymological sense of this adjective, as always separable from every relationship and synthesis, tearing itself away from the very justice where this exteriority enters. The absolute—an abusive word—could probably take place concretely and have meaning only in the phenomenology, or in the rupture of phenomenology, which the face of the other calls forth.

The face of the Other—*under* all the particular forms of expression where the Other, already in a character's skin, plays a role—is just as much *pure expression*, an extradition without defense or cover, precisely the extreme rectitude of a *facing*, which in this nudity is an exposure unto death: nudity, destitution, passivity, and pure vulnerability. Such is the face as the very *mortality* of the other person.

But through this mortality, which is also an assignation and obligation that concern the ego—which "concern me"—there is a "facing up" of authority, as if the invisible death to which the face of the other person is exposed were, for the Ego that approaches it, *his* business, implicating him before his guilt or innocence, or at least without his intentional guilt. The Ego as hostage of the other person is precisely called to answer for this death. This responsibility is for the Other in the ego, independent of every engagement ever taken by this ego and of all that would have ever been accessible to its initiative and its freedom, independent of everything that in the Other could have "regarded" this ego. But here, through the face of the Other, through his mortality, everything that in the Other does not regard me, "regards me." Responsibility for the Other—the face signifying to me "thou shalt not kill," and consequently also "you are responsible for the life of this absolutely other other"—is responsibility for the unique one. The "unique one" means the *loved one*, love being the condition of the very possibility of uniqueness.

The condition or noncondition of the hostage is accentuated in the Ego approaching the neighbor. But so too is its *election*, the unicity of he who does not allow himself to be replaced. Such a one is no longer the "individual within a genus," called *Ego*, not "a particular case" of the "Ego in general." It is the ego that speaks in the first person, like the one Dostoyevsky has say "I am the most guilty of all," in the obligation of each for each, as the most obligated— the unique one. Such is the one whose obligation with regard to the Other is also infinite, who, without self-interrogation about reciprocity, without posing questions about the Other at the approach of his face, is never done with the neighbor.

The "relationship" from the ego to the other is thus asymmetrical, without noematic correlation of any thematizable presence. It is an awakening to the other person— the first arrival in his *proximity* as neighbor—irreducible to knowledge, even were one called before the plurality of others, through the exigencies of justice. It is a thought that is not an adequation to the other, who no longer measures up to me, and who precisely in his unicity is refractory to every measure. But nonetheless it is a non-in-difference to the other, where love breaks the equilibrium of the equanimous soul. It puts into question the ego's natural position as subject, its perseverance—the perseverance of its good conscience—in its being. It puts into question its *conatus essendi*, the stubbornness of its being [*étant*]. Here is an indiscreet—or "unjust"—presence, which is perhaps already an issue in "The Anaximander Fragment," such as

Heidegger interprets it in *Holzwege*. It puts into question the "positivity" of the *esse* in its *presence*, signifying, bluntly, encroachment and usurpation! Did not Heidegger—despite all he intends to teach about the priority of the "thought of being"—here run up against the original significance of ethics? The offense done to the Other by being's "good conscience" is already an offense done to the stranger, the widow, and the orphan,[2] who, in the face of the Other, regard the ego.[3]

TIME AND SOCIALITY

I have attempted a "phenomenology" of sociality starting from the face of the other person—from proximity—by understanding in its rectitude a voice that commands before all mimicry and verbal expression, in the mortality of the face, from the bottom of this weakness. It commands me to not remain indifferent to this death, to not let the Other die alone, that is, to answer for the life of the other person, at the risk of becoming an accomplice in that person's death. The facing-up of the Other, in his rectitude, would signify both the precariousness of the Other and an authority lacking to a simply logical *alterity*, which, as the counterpart of the identity of facts and concepts, distinguishes one from another, or reciprocally opposes the notions of them, by contradiction or contrariety. The alterity of the Other is the extreme point of the "thou shalt not kill" and, in me, the fear of all the violence and usurpation that

[2]See *Time and the Other*, note 64, above.

[3]Levinas: But what an encumbrance of language or what an ambiguity in the ego! Here it is that we speak of the ego as a concept even though in each ego the "first person" is unicity and not the individuation of a genus. The ego, if one can say it, is *me*. It is not there where one speaks about it, but there where it speaks in the first person: the ego evading the concept despite the power that the concept regains over it as soon as one speaks about this evasion, this unicity, or this Election.

my existing, despite the innocence of its intentions, risks committing. Here is the risk of occupying—from the *Da* of my *Dasein*—the place of an Other and, thus, in the concrete, of exiling him, dooming him to a miserable condition in some "third" or "fourth" world, bringing him death. Thus an unlimited responsibility would emerge in this fear for the other person, a responsibility with which one is never done, which does not cease with the neighbor's utmost extremity—despite the merciless and realistic formula of the physician who "condemns" a patient—even if the responsibility amounts to nothing more than responding "here I am," in the impotent confrontation with the Other's death, or in the shame of surviving, to ponder the memory of one's faults. This is so despite all the modern denunciations of the inefficiency and the easiness of "bad conscience"! It is a responsibility that, without doubt, keeps the secret of sociality, whose total gravity—be it vain to the limit—is called "love of the neighbor"—that is, the very possibility of the unicity of the unique one (beyond the particularity of the individual in a genus).[4] It is a love without concupiscence, but as irrefragable as death.

Sociality is not to be confused with some lapse or privation that would have taken place in the unity of the One, where "perfection" and the unity of coincidence, having fallen into separation, would aspire to their integrity. From the bottom of the natural perseverance in the being of a being, assured of its *right to be*—to the point of ignoring its concept and problem—from the heart of a logically indiscernible identity—because it rests on itself and dispenses with every distinctive sign that would be necessary for identification—from the bottom of the identity of the Ego precisely and, against the perseverance of good conscience, and implicating this restful identity—arises the anxiety of a responsibility I have not decided to take upon myself, for I

[4]On the shift from individuality to uniqueness through love of the neighbor, see F. Rosenzweig, *The Star of Redemption*, pp. 211-218.

have not identified my own identity, and am awakened by the soundless and imperative language that the face of the Other speaks (without having the compelling force of the visible). Responsibility is anterior to deliberation and is that to which I have thus been exposed and dedicated before being dedicated to myself. Is this a vow or a devotion?

IMMEMORIAL PAST

Responsibility is anterior to all the logical deliberation summoned by reasoned decision. Deliberation would already be the reduction of the face of the Other to a representation, to the objectivity of the visible, to its compelling force, which belongs to the world. The anteriority of responsibility is not that of an a priori idea interpreted starting from reminiscence—that is, referred to perception and the glimpsed intemporal presence starting from the ideality of the idea or the eternity of a presence that does not pass, and whose duration or dia-chrony of time would be only a dissimulation, decrease, deformation, or privation, in finite human consciousness.

In the ethical anteriority of responsibility, for-the-other, in its priority over deliberation, there is a past irreducible to a presence that it must have been. This past is without reference to an identity naively—or naturally—assured of its right to presence, where everything must have begun. In this responsibility I am thrown back toward what has never been my fault or my deed, toward what has never been in my power or in my freedom, toward what has never been my presence, and has never come into memory. There is an ethical significance in this responsibility, this an-archic responsibility, without the present recalling any engagement. It is the significance of a past that concerns me, that "regards me," and is "my business" outside of all reminiscence, re-tention, re-presentation, or reference to a remembered present. The significance of an immemorial past, starting from responsibility for the other person, comes in the heteronomy of an order. Such is my *nonintentional* participation in the history of humanity, in the past of others, who "regard me." The dia-chrony of a past that does not gather into re-presentation is at the bottom of the concreteness of the time that is the time of my responsibility for the Other.

Responsibility for the Other does not come down to a thought going back to an a priori idea, previously given to and rediscovered by the "I think." The natural *conatus essendi* of a sovereign ego is put into question by the death or the mortality of the Other, in the ethical vigilance through which the sovereignty of the "ego" can recognize itself as "hateful," and its "place in the sun" as the "image and beginning of the usurpation of the whole world."[5] The responsibility for the Other signified as an order in the neighbor's face is not, in me, the simple modality of "transcendental apperception." The order concerns me without it being possible for me to go back to the thematic presence of a being that would be the cause or the willing of this commandment. As I have said, it is again not a question here of receiving an order by first perceiving it and then subjecting oneself to it in a decision taken after having deliberated about it. In the proximity of the face, the subjection precedes the reasoned decision to assume the order that it bears. The passivity of this subjection is not like the receptivity of the intellectual operation that returns to itself in the act of assuming, in the spontaneity of welcome and grasp. Here the absolute foreignness of an unassumable alterity is refractory to its assimilation into presence, is foreign to the apperception of the "I think" that always assumes what strikes it by re-presenting it. The dia-chrony

[5]This reference to Pascal (*Pensées*, Bruncschvicg 295/Lafuma 112), also appears as an epigram to Levinas' *Otherwise than Being or Beyond Essence*.

of the past is unequalled. The subjection preceding the understanding of the order attests to or measures an infinite authority. And this is so without the future being given in the to-come [à-venir], where the grasp of an anticipation—or a protention—would come to obscure the dia-chrony of time, which bears the authority of an imperative.

The past articulates itself—or "thinks itself"—without recourse to the memory, without a return to "living presents," and is not made up of re-presentations. The past signifies starting from an irrecusable responsibility, which devolves on the ego and precisely is significant to it as a commandment, without, for all that, reverting back to an engagement that it would have had to have taken in some forgotten present. The past has the signification of an inveterate obligation, older than any engagement, taking the whole of its meaning in the imperative that commands the ego by way of the Other's face. This categorical imperative is without regard—so to say—for any freely taken decision that would "justify" responsibility, and without regard for any alibi. The immemorial past signified without ever having been present, signified starting from the responsibility "for the other," where obedience is the proper mode of attending to the commandment. Attending to a commandment is thus not the recall of some prior generous dispositions toward the Other, which are forgotten or secret, and belong to the constitution of the *ego* and are awakened as an *a priori* by the Other's face. The understanding of a commandment as already an obedience is not a decision resulting from a deliberation—be it dialectical—opening out in the Other's face, where the prescription would derive its necessity from a theoretical conclusion. The power of the commandment would not just signify a force greater than mine. The commandment here would precisely not proceed from a force. It comes—by way of an Other's face—as renouncing constraint, as renouncing its force and whatever is all-powerful. Its authority is intract-

able to the determinism of formal and ontological structures. Its heteronomy does not inevitably signify enslavement. It is the heteronomy of an irrecusable authority,
despite the necessities of being and the imperturbable pace
that it follows, careful of its very being. This is precisely the
whole novelty of ethics where disobedience and transgres-
sion do not refute authority and goodness, and which, impotent but sovereign, returns in bad conscience. The latter
does not attest to an incomplete thought that would be visible in its generous nonviolence, nor to the immaturity of a
childish reason. It would signify—beyond the contribu-
tions of memory, deliberation, and violent force—an exceptional sonority which, in its irreducibility, suggests the
eventuality of the word of God.

Pure Future

Signification comes from an authority that is significant
after and despite my death, signifying to the finite ego, to the
ego doomed to death, a meaningful order significant beyond this death. This is not, to be sure, some promise of
resurrection, but an obligation that death does not absolve
and a future contrasting strongly with the synchronizable
time of re-presentation, and with the time offered to intentionality, where the *I think* would keep the last word, in-
vesting what is imposed upon its powers of assuming.

There is responsibility for the other right up to dying for
the other! This is how the alterity of the Other—distant and
near—affects, through my own responsibility, the utmost
present, which, for the identity of my *I think*, gathers itself
together again, as does all my duration, into presence or
representation, but which is also the end of all egological
provision of meaning by intentional thought, an end
which, in my "being-for-death," this provision would al-

ready doom, and which is anticipated in the unbreakable immanence of its conscious existing. In the paroxysm of the proximity of the neighbor, the face of the other person—which one thus has reason not to interpret as a re-presentation—communicates its own way—imperative—of signifying a meaning to a mortal ego, through the eventual exhaustion of its egological *Sinngebung* and the anticipated shamelessness of all the meaning that proceeds from this *Sinngebung*. There is in the Other a meaning and an obliga-tion that oblige me beyond my death! The futuration of the future does not reach me as a to-come [*à-venir*], as the hori-zon of my anticipations or pro-tentions. Must one not, in this *imperative* signification of the future that concerns me as a non-in-difference to the other person, as my responsi-bility for the stranger—must one not, in this rupture of the natural order of being, understand what is—improperly—called super-natural? Is it not to understand an order that would be the word of God or, still more exactly, the very coming of God to the idea and its insertion into a vocabulary—whence comes the "recognizing" and naming of God in every possible Revelation? The futuration of the future is not a "proof of God's existence," but "the fall of God into meaning." This is the singular intrigue of the du-ration of time, beyond its signification as presence or as re-ducible to presence, up to Saint Augustine himself—time as the to-God [*à-Dieu*] of theology!

Responsibility for the Other, responding to the Other's death, vows itself to an alterity that is no longer within the province of re-presentation. This way of being avowed—or this devotion—is time. It remains a relationship to the other as other, and not a reduction of the other to the same. It is transcendence. In the finitude of time the "being-toward-death" of *Being and Time* sketches out—despite all the re-newals of handed down philosophy that this brilliant book brings—the meaningful remains enclosed within the im-manence of the *Jemeinigkeit* of the *Dasein* that *has to be* and that thus—in spite of the denunciation of being as presence—still belongs to a philosophy of presence. Does not responsibility for the Other's death—the fear for the Other that no longer enters into the Heideggerian phenomenology of emotion, *Befindlichkeit*—consist in understanding, in the finite being of the mortal ego starting from the Other's face, the meaning of a *future* beyond what happens to me, beyond what, for an ego, is to-come? One would thus not have gone to the end of thought and meaningfulness in dying. The meaningful continues beyond my death. Is it still necessary to call this non-in-difference of responsibility for the Other by the name *relationship*, even though the terms of every relationship are already—or still—within the ideality of system—simultaneous? And is not dia-chrony—more formal than transcendence, but also more significant—found to be irreducible to all noetic-noematic correlation through the concreteness of the responsibility of one for the death of the other?

TO-GOD [*A-DIEU*]

Subjection to the order that ordains man—the ego—to answer for the other is, perhaps, the harsh name of love. Love here is no longer what this compromised word of our literature and our hypocrisies expresses, but the very fact of the approach of the unique one and, consequently, of the absolutely *other*, piercing what merely *shows* itself—that is to say, what remains the "individual of a genus." Love here implies the whole order—or the whole disorder—of the psychic or the subjective, which would no longer be the abyss of the arbitrary where ontological meaning is lost, but the very place that is indispensable to the promotion of the *logical* category of *unicity*, beyond the distinction between the universal and the individual.

This subjection is to an absolute order, to the authority par excellence, or to the authority of excellence or of the Good. Is it not the very occasion—or the "circumstances"— where, contrasting strongly with the perseverance of a *being* in its being, authority takes its full sense? It brings neither promise nor relief, but the absoluteness of an exigency. It is the Word of God, perhaps, providing God is only named starting from this authority where he merely comes to the idea. The "unknown" God does not take shape in a theme, and is exposed, through this very transcendence— through this very nonpresence—to the denials of atheism. But is it certain that thematization is appropriate to the Infinite, that vision is the supreme excellence of the spirit, and that through the egoism and egology of being, it is the original mode of thought?

In the idea of the Infinite, thought thinks more than it can contain and, according to Descartes' Third Meditation, God is thought in humankind. Is it not like a noesis without a noema? And the concreteness of responsibility, in its extra-ordinary and nonencompassable future, is it not ordained through its Word in the face of the Other?

The subjection that precedes deliberation about an imperative, measures, so to speak, or attests to, an infinite authority, but also an extreme refusal of coerciveness, a nonviolent refusing to be forced, refusing every retreat from its transcendence and all its Infinity! Is the retreat from transcendence and indeclinable authority already the dia-chrony of time? Infinite and indeclinable authority does not prevent disobedience, which leaves time—that is to say, freedom. Such is the ambiguity of authority and nonviolence. The human as bad conscience is the Gordian knot of this ambiguity of the idea of the Infinite, of the Infinite as idea. Bad conscience is not only the sign of an incomplete reason, or already the appeasement and the precipitate justification of sin, or already all the good conscience of hypocrisy, but also the opportunity for holiness in a society of the just, without good conscience and, in the inextinguishable concern for justice, assent to the rigor of human justice.

DEFORMALIZATION OF TIME

The signification of a past that has not been my present and does not concern my reminiscence, and the signification of a future that commands me in mortality or in the face of the Other—beyond my powers, my finitude, and my being-doomed-to-death—no longer articulate the representable time of immanence and its historical present. Its dia-chrony, the "difference" of diachrony, does not signify pure rupture, but a non-in-difference and concordance that are no longer founded on the unity of transcendental apperception, the most formal of forms, which through reminiscence and hope joins time up again in re-presenting it, but betrays it. I am not going to speak, however, about these concordances of dia-chrony, about the to-God of time, or about its prophecy, whose ultimate concreteness is time itself in its patience. Its "adventure" or "intrigue," which I have above all tried to distinguish from the presence of being, and which I have approached starting from the ethical in the human, can neither be constituted nor better said starting from any category or "existential."[6] All the figures and words that try to express it—such as "transcendence" or "beyond"—are already derived from it. The *to-God* is neither the thematization of theologies, nor a finality, which goes to a term and not to the Infinite, nor the eschatology preoccupied with ultimate ends or with promises rather than with obligations with regard to humans.

[6]The distinction between "categorical" analysis and "existential" analysis is fundamental to Heidegger's *Being and Time,* where the former applies to *objects,* as Kant understood, and the latter applies to the being of *Dasein.* See Heidegger, *Being and Time,* section 12, pp. 78–86.

But the prepositions themselves, including the *to* and the *pro*, are already only metaphors of time, and could not serve in its constitution.

It was important to me above all to speak in this study about how, in the human intrigue, past, future, and present are tied together in time, without this resulting from a simple degradation that the unity of the One could have—I do not know how—undergone, dispersing itself, in the *movement* that since—or according to—Aristotle was acceded to time in its diachrony. In such a view the unity of time would lose itself in the flow of instants, to find itself again—without truly finding itself—in re-presentation, where the past gathers together instants by way of the memory's images, and the future by way of installments and promises. But I have sought for time as the deformalization of the most formal form that is, the unity of the *I think.* Deformalization is that with which Bergson, Rosenzweig, and Heidegger, each in his own way, have opened the problematic of modern thought, by starting from a concreteness "older" than the pure form of time: the freedom of invention and novelty (despite the persistance of the kinetic image of a *flow*) in Bergson; the biblical conjunction of "Creation, Revelation, and Redemption" in Rosenzweig; and the "nearness to things," *Geworfenheit,* and *Sein-zum-Tode* (despite the still kinetic *ex* of the *exstases*) in Heidegger. Is it forbidden to also recall that in *The Two Sources of Morality and Religion,*[7] the duration of *Time and Free Will*[8] and *Matter and Memory,*[9] thought as *élan vital* in *Crea-*

[7]Henri Bergson, *The Two Sources of Morality and Religion,* translated by R. Audra and C. Brereton (Garden City, New York: Doubleday & Company, 1935). First French publication: 1932. [See, especially, pp. 98–99.]

[8]Henri Bergson, *Time and Free Will: An Essay on the Immediate Data of Consciousness,* translated by F. Pogson (New York: Harper & Row, 1960). First French publication: 1913.

[9]Henri Bergson, *Matter and Memory,* translated by N. Paul and W. Palmer (Garden City, New York: Doubleday & Company, 1959). First French publication: 1896.

tive Evolution,[10] signifies love of the neighbor and what I have called "to-God"? But do I have the right to make this comparison, notwithstanding all the teachings of the half-century that separates us from the publication of *The Two Sources of Morality and Religion?*

What seems in fact to be opened, after the steps attempted to think time starting from the face of the Other, where "God comes to us in the idea," as an authority that there commands indeclinably, but also refuses to compel and commands entirely while renouncing the all-powerful, is the necessity to think time in the devotion of a theology without theodicy. To be sure, this religion is impossible to propose to the Other, and consequently is impossible to preach. Contrary to a religion that feeds on representations, it does not begin with a promise. Is it necessary to again recognize in it the difficult piety—all the certainties and personal risks—of the twentieth century, after the horrors of its genocides and its holocaust?

To be sure, one can ask if the time of promises ever stands at the beginning elsewhere than in pedagogy, and if the service without promises is not the only one to merit—and even to accomplish—promises. But these two questions seem already suspect of preaching.

---

[10]Henri Bergson, *Creative Evolution*, translated by A. Mitchell (New York: Random House, 1944). First French publication: 1911.

The Old and the New (1980)

T hat the New and Renewal are peaks of human life, that one can define the human by the desire for the new and by the capacity for renewal—is perhaps a basic truth, but a truth. One desires renewal, independently of any error committed, unless the pure persistence in the Same is not already an error. One loves the new, whatever distrust *studium rerum novarum*,[1] the worry about fashion, the search for originality at any price—and all the degrees of degradation to which this love lends itself—can inspire in our natural conservatism, which, precisely, would merely be natural and nature in us. Exposed to aging, to an outrage more offensive perhaps than death,[2] to an outrage, in any case, that is highly offensive, in which the human coagulates into an identity, sinking into itself, the Desire for the new in us is a Desire for *the other*; it distinguishes our being from *existing*, which is self sufficient, and which, *conatus essendi*, perseveres in existing, holding, above all, to this very existing. In the natural throbbing of the being of beings, the *human* would thus be the rupture

---

[1]"The eagerness for new things."

[2]Levinas: For death—even if it should, according to a cynical expression, "stop the music" is, in "the identity" of the ego, the passage to a "wholly other" or, at least, the cessation of the "Same." Franz Rosenzweig, in his last letter calls it "the point of all points." Cf. Franz Rosenzweig; *Briefe und Tagebucher*, vol. II (The Hague, Martinus Nijhoff, 1979)p. 1237.

of this ontological rhythm. How is this possible? What does it mean over and above its negativity? Therein lies the interest of the problem of the *old* and the *new,* of the determination of these notions, of the event and the bearing of genuine renewal.

We will begin with the commonplace notion of the new and the old, one that refers to the *present* of a linear and formal time. We will then examine it in terms of the idea of the *modern,* on the horizon of the Hegelian philosophy of History and the intellectual tradition of the West that this philosophy sums up. Bergsonism, which seems to interrupt this tradition, provides us valuable suggestions and encouragement to formulate in the last part of our exposition a notion of the New linked to that of absolute alterity and, thus, to transcendence.

CHRONOLOGY AND THE PRESENT

According to common sense, the *old* and the *new* designate the place that the elements of our experience and our dispositions take within the line of time. What is new is what is present—or on the point of presenting itself. The elements of experience and those of dispositions are old to the extent that they withdraw from presence, which constitutes the zero point in the scale of time: the point where what is comes to be—or is on the point of being produced. The present is the future making itself present. Time, the pure form of experience, thus designates the ordering of phenomena, each relative to the others, each more or less recent than others. The phenomenon's content is of no importance to its newness or oldness. "Affective tonalities" that qualitatively mark the "phenomena" are added to this chronological ordering, an ordering that would be produced without regard for the quality of the phenomena: the old is the habitual, the banal, the "well-known" known, the boring; the new can have charm, bears the "unforeseen," is interesting, promising or fresh; conversely, the old is familiar, sure, already dear, always "touching"; the new is upsetting, menacing or hostile.

Viewed under this formal time perspective, everything *new* ages. In the temporal succession, reduced to pure chronology, nothing stays absolutely new. Absolute newness is instantaneous in the "now" already labile and already depreciated by the future horizon, by the future in view of a new virtually newer than the new. The new sinks into the "older and older."

But already a point of view open to the content of what is lived intervenes in this experience of the old and the new, which believes or wants itself to be purely chronological, and thus disturbs the relativity of pure form. A certain ordering is outlined between the lived contents—or in the experience of these contents. It dominates that of simple succession. "Histories" are superimposed onto it. A finality or a system of elements that are not integrated by chronology is affirmed between things or between dispositions. These can appear new in relation to the orderings with which they contrast; or, to the contrary, what is arranged under the orderings that are outlined—thus taking on a meaning—can seem new in relation to the monotony of the pure throbbing of time, thereby marking a progression which is independent of the march of time. The revival of an old element in a meaningful ordering that breaks away from the course of experience would be a renewal of this element, which, according to the solely chronological order, belonged to the past. In the nostalgia for origins, the past returns, in the imagination, more new than it was in its present, and purely temporal novelties exist that are straightaway worn and old.

HISTORY AND THE MODERN

Through the systems of finality—which are multiple and in some way contingent—that appear in our experience, and, according to which particular events or lived contents, entirely while succeeding themselves, are arranged through their qualitative tenor into various histories, both short and long, where the new is measured by its conformity to these histories by its place in them, or by their interruption, Western humanity has been conscious of a single and universal historical ordering, one that unfolds with a view to a culmination. But no doubt this is so starting with a certain *content* which intrinsically bears the signification *new,* a signification recognized under the adjective *modern.*

The modern is constituted by the consciousness of a certain definitively acquired freedom. Everything is possible and everything is permitted, for nothing, absolutely speaking, precedes this freedom. It is a freedom that does not bow before any factual state, thus negating the "already done" and living only from the new. But it is a freedom with which no memory interferes, a freedom upon which no past weighs. Everything *old,* which is at once superseded and revalorized in the modern, leads toward it. It acquires the plenitude of its sense there, as a noncircumventable and preparatory stage to this novel state, which the antiquity of the world, its anteriority to experience, does not come to compromise and render old. This situation makes possible the fact—for freedom—of keeping to the element of knowledge, thereby comprehending the world and the past in terms of *being* which knowledge assimilates, thus mastering the alterity which is manifest in being. According to our European tradition, all spirituality is indeed knowledge: everything that comes about in the human psychism finishes through knowledge and through self-knowledge. All that is lived and legitimately called experience is converted into received lessons. Relationships with the neighbor, the social group, and God, would still be a collective or religious *experience*. It is doubtlessly this knowledge, implicit in every human adventure, that justifies the wide use Descartes makes of the term *cogito*. And this first person verb says the encompassing unity well, where all knowledge suffices unto itself and is organized into a system. As knowledge, thought bears upon the thinkable called being; bearing upon being, it is outside of itself, to be sure, but remains, marvelously, in itself. The exteriority, alterity, or antiquity, of what is "already there" in the known, is taken up again into immanence: the known is at once *the other* and the *property* of thought. Nothing preexists: one learns as if one *created*. Reminiscence and imagination secure the synchrony and unity of what, in experience bound to time, was doomed to the difference between the old and the new. The new as modern is the fully arranged state of the self and world.

But the arrangement is not immediate: freedom is not a spontaneous agency. Freedom is the *positive* power of modern man, exerted upon nature and human events; consequently freedom is lived essentially in correlation with the development of science and the techniques that civilization brings. Science extends to the whole of the real and thus to man himself. Human sciences appear which are characterized by a rupture with the immediate givens of consciousness[3] and with naively performed introspection. Whether through critical analyses of social facts or through psychoanalytical studies, modernity and its freedom are always in correlation with the institutional existence of science, methods, and manipulations of the given. Suspicion is cast upon immediate givens! Freedom is tied to the

[3]This expression, in French, *"les données immédiates de la conscience,"* recalls Henri Bergson's work, *Essai sur les données immédiates de la conscience* (1889), translated into English by F. L. Pogson under the title *Time and Free Will: An Essay on the Immediate Data of Consciousness*.

exigency of an extreme lucidity, which then opens up an
era of suspicion'—according to the felicitous formula of
Paul Ricoeur—upon the straightforward testimonies and
the wishes of persons. Suspicion weighs upon the intentions and meanings which at first seem to exhaust the
words and gestures of persons. *A science behind consciousness is always necessary,* even if the modernity that exerts this
control wants and calls for *self consciousness.* From this
comes, notably, the historical relativity of moral values,
subject to a "genealogy" of morals, and the denunciation
of appearances and ideologies.

"Everything is permitted"—universal absolution is assured, but is tied to the necessity which would have to
grant this freedom in the Other too, and, thus, as a freedom inseparable from the political philosophies which
substitute themselves for meditations on the self and for
"inner life." The novelty of the modern is understood as
the supreme freedom referring to all possibilities, to all the
acquisitions of European civilization, reuniting all types of
knowledge, and interpreted as progress toward absolute
knowledge knowing itself absolute and synonymous with
Spirit. Does not time itself—which for everyday consciousness bears all events, and renders possible the play of the
old and the new, the very aspiration for the new in the aging of all actuality—lose for modern humanity its innova-
ting virtue and its peremptory powers? What can modern
humanity expect from a future which it believes is held in
the present of its absolute knowledge, where nothing is
any longer exterior to consciousness?

It is Hegelian philosophy that affirms with rigor and
vigor—which would be characteristics of reason itself—this
notion of modernity, where the old fits in with the new in
the *true* or in the eternal, where the temporality of time is
only this progressive reconciliation, and where the inner
perception of progression in time is the discovery of history. Philosophic knowledge would not be the luxury of
some interesting reflection of reality. It is the culminating

moment of this reality itself that is reunited in it to make a totality; even though the special sciences that it outstrips link up again with limited parts of the real and signify a partialness and a partiality, a finitude—despite their pretension of having the last word, which is still naive for the moment where they are placed. Philosophy is guided by the idea of the totality of the real, of its truth beyond the old and the new. In passing beyond the sciences and perceptions and, in them, the partial aspects of this totality of the True, it does not exclude what it passes beyond as false. The old is the one-sided that is encompassed in the whole, finding its bearings in the novelty of the modern. Behind spontaneous consciousness, true thought precisely manifests the universality of the real, beyond the facets and pretensions of provisional truths. Rationality is the encompassing of the new: an attitude taken in its regard, the negation of the difference which at first seemed to separate it from the old. To think the new is to raise it to the True. Assimilating and encompassing thought goes beyond everything peremptory. Time is not a succession of novelties which are made old and aged, but a history where everything comes and goes into a time progressively constituting the truth. It is an edification of the true whose completion is like a novelty which no longer has to yield to any other which is newer, an absolute novelty which does not pass. The novelty of the modern is not, to be sure, the end of everything unknown, but an epoch where the unknown to be discovered can no longer surprise thought with its new alterity. Thought is already fully conscious of itself and of all the dimensions of what is reasonable in reality. For thought, everything is consummated.

DURATION AND CHANGE

Hegel is obviously considerable. But one can put into question the novelty of the modern as it is lived, even if it is difficult to contest the accuracy of the image Hegel gives to human consciousness' ascent to the zenith. One can ask if the concept of novelty that the Hegelian analysis promotes answers definitively to the human desire for the new and for renewal. This desire, which goes right to the excessive-ness of the dream of eternal youth, is nonetheless not mad, but belongs to those several exigencies wherein man infi-nitely surpasses man. One can ask if the human coincides with knowledge. One can call late nineteenth century phi-losophies to witness; one thinks of Nietzsche, and of Bergson, who is so unjustly forgotten today. One stresses certain moments of Heideggerian thought. One must refer to all the actual experience of our twentieth century, which is the proof of an unbalanced world, to the world wars, to the totalitarianisms of right and left, to the holocaust, pro-totype of all genocides—to all this barbarism of the human or inhuman face. There is a crisis of human freedom, power, and knowledge, a reversal of technological power into enslavement. There are all the unremitting and already well known critiques of the modern novelties, which are all the more serious as they are not followed up with any exal-tation of past values. No return to the old could reasonably be preached. Has not the world completed by knowledge, where in the final account novelty only stands out as a menace, grown old in this heavy *fin-de-siècle* conscious-ness?

One is then led to ask if the *relation to the new* such as it has dominated our Western tradition, where Hegel has been its supreme speculative expression and where re-newal culminates in modernity, i.e., domination as knowl-edge of new forms, of *other* forms,—as Hegel admirably ex-presses when he seeks the identity of the *same* and the *other*, or when, from the same and the other, he precisely seeks identity—one can ask if such a relation to newness conforms to the human desire for renewal, if, in the knowl-edge where novelty is dealt with, the other, the new, is still

sought in its alterity. Against the encompassing, accumu-
lating and organizing consciousness of the system through
knowledge, against the tendency to equalize the new, as if
it were only an unknown to know and not the other to desire in its unassimilable alterity—that is to say, to love rather
than to equalize by knowledge—against this pan-logical
civilization Bergsonism brings to bear an inestimable message. It perceives the essential—if one can say—of the psychism in change, in an unceasing passage to the other
which does not stop at any identity; it teaches us time in
primordial change, not as a "mobile image of immobile
eternity"—what it has been in the whole history of Western
thought: simply the forfeiture of the permanence of being,
a privation of eternity—but as the original excellence and
the very superiority of mind [esprit].

Bergson draws back from the ontological supremacy of
Identity and the concept of Substance that expresses it in
the traditional thought of being, which, according to him,
would have gone on alongside the very duration of time. Is
it still necessary today to introduce to an educated public,
but one that manages to forget the unforgettable, the
Bergsonian distinction between the time of our everyday
lives and the time of inner life or duration? On the one
hand, there is common sense time—which essentially remains that of science—the measurable time of our watches,
Aristotle's time understood as the numbering of movement, that is, time which is accessible starting from its spatial expression and measurement by chronometers,
whether they be watches or clepsydras,[4] a time homoge-
nous like space, made up of invariable instants which re-
peat themselves, where all novelty would be reducible to
these old elements, a spatialized time, the time of action in
space, the time of technique, which conforms to the views
and concepts of the understanding. And, on the other
hand, there is duration which is pure change, without re-

[4]Water clocks.

trieving any identical substrate beneath this change. It becomes unthinkable for the understanding's conceptuality,
but is immediate life as a preconceptual time that one can
rediscover through an effort called intuition. Intuition is a
return to oneself and to the autonomous upsurge of unceasing novelty before its reduction to like instants, which
are the fruits of the abstraction necessary for action. Novelty would thus be the very reality of the real, the being of a
being, as one would say today,[5] where no instant is isolated
in its identity.

Duration, in its very change, is indivisible like an élan.
And if one starts with the idea of the instant, borrowed
from spatialized time, duration would be an interpenetra-
tion of instants, a time where each instant is "heavy" with
its entire past and "big" with its entire future, where nothing, consequently, is ever definitive, where nothing reduces to its oldness, where the destiny of an actually lived
life recommences at each instant, receiving a new sense
starting from the inimitable novelty of the present which
opens upon an unforeseeable future. The youth or unend-
ing spring of consciousness is for Bergson equivalent to the
freedom of humankind's profound being. Bergson writes:

> Intelligence starts ordinarily from the immobile, and
> reconstructs movement as best it can with immobili-
> ties in juxtaposition. Intuition starts from movement,
> posits it, or rather perceives it as reality itself, and
> sees in immobility only an abstract moment, a snap-
> shot taken by our mind, of a mobility. Intelligence or-
> dinarily concerns itself with things, meaning by that,

[5]Levinas: In fact there would be a liberation with regard to the ontology
of the *being* in Bergsonism, beyond its obvious critique of immobile sub-
stantiality. The new, for it, is not simply a new *quiddity* filling time.
Thought in the very temporalization of time, in Bergson the qualitative is a
way of being, a *how* rather than a quiddity. And through this, in its conception of duration, the thematization of the future "being-of-the-being"
appears in Bergsonism as in *Being and Time.*

with the static, and makes of change an accident which is supposedly superadded. For intuition the essential is change: as for the thing, as intelligence understands it, it is a cutting which has been made out of the becoming and set up by our mind as a substitute for the whole. Thought ordinarily pictures to itself the new as a new arrangement of pre-existing elements; nothing is ever lost for it, nothing is ever created. Intuition, bound up to a duration which is growth, perceives in it an uninterrupted continuity of unforeseeable novelty; it sees, it knows that the mind draws from itself more than it has, that spirituality consists in just that, and that reality, impregnated with spirit [esprit], is creation.[6]

And bit further on:

A new idea may be clear because it presents to us, simply arranged in a new order, elementary ideas which we already possessed. Our intelligence, finding only the old in the new, feels itself on familiar ground; it is at ease, it "understands." Such is the clarity we desire, are looking for, and for which we are always most grateful to whoever presents it to us. There is another kind that we submit to, and which, moreover, imposes itself only with time. It is the clarity of the radically new and absolutely simple idea, which catches as it were an intuition.[7]

[6]Levinas: See The Creative Mind, (translated by M. Andison; New York: Philosophical Library, Inc., 1946) pp. 34–35. [La Pensée et le Mouvant (Paris: Presses Universitaires de France, 1934) pp. 38–39.] The Husserlian analysis of time answers to this essential message of Bergson on time, in a way that is a meeting of two independent minds. In Husserl, too, there is a rupture with the static notion of the separable instant, there is retention and protention, interpenetrated thoughts, and the iteration of these temporal "intentionalities": retention of retention and protention of protention, etc. There is also the absolute novelty of the proto-impression occurring without genesis.

[7]Levinas: The Creative Mind, p. 35. [La Pensée et le Mouvant, pp. 39–40.]

It is important to underline the importance of
Bergsonism for the entire problematic of contemporary philosophy; it is an essential stage of the movement which
puts into question the ontological confines of spirituality. It
no longer returns to the assimilating act of consciousness,
to the reduction of all novelty—of all alterity—to what in
one way or another thought already supported, to the reduction of every other [Autre] to the Same. It is no longer
what one could call the thought of the equal, a rationality
revealing a reality which keeps to the very measure of a
thought. "Duration will be revealed as it is—unceasing creation, the uninterrupted up-surge of novelty."[8] It is the
emergence of the always new, of the unequal. Priority is
given to the relations traditional philosophy always treated
as secondary and subordinate. "They [most philosophers]
treat succession as a coexistence which has failed to be
achieved, and duration as a non-eternity. That is why, in
spite of all their efforts, they cannot succeed in conceiving
the radically new and unforeseeable."[9] In this reversal—the
priority of duration over permanence—there is access to
novelty, an access independent of the ontology of the
Same.

In this new analysis of time one can catch sight of something else than an anthropological peculiarity: with
Bergsonism one can think the human as the explosion of
being in duration. The human would be the original place
of rupture and would have a metaphysical bearing: it
would be the very advent of mind [esprit]. Mind is no
longer absolute knowledge as consciousness of self and
equality to self, but the emergence of the new as duration.
The anthropological upsurge of duration would delineate,
before logic, the horizons of intelligibility, as later, in
Heidegger, do the ecstases of temporality, which are tied to
being-in-the-world, to Geworfenheit and to being-for-death.

[8]Levinas: The Creative Mind, p. 18. [La Pensée et le Mouvant, p. 16.]
[9]Levinas: The Creative Mind, p. 18. [La Pensée et le Mouvant, p. 17.]

These horizons of meaning are "older" and more "original" than the structures of scientific time, and are that from which—as in Heidegger—scientific time would be derived and abstracted.

DIACHRONY AND TRANSCENDENCE

Do these Bergsonian openings onto the priority of the *new*, defined on the basis of duration, definitively overcome what the very notion of consciousness—whose immediate givens Bergson scrutinizes—entails of the assimilative? Is not Bergsonian intuition as consciousness—be it pre-reflexive, as the spontaneous and immediate "actually lived life"—confusion and coincidence and, thus, an experience still rediscovering its standards in a worked over alterity? The aging of the new! Does intuition constitute the modality of thought, within which the alterity of the *new* would explode, immaculate and untouchable as alterity or absolute newness, the absolute itself in the etymological sense of the term? Does the thought which relates to the new allow it to maintain its novelty and to stand the wear and tear? Even though, coextensive with consciousness, thought by itself is knowledge, grasp, and preoccupation with being: inter-ested—*the alterity* of the new is reduced to its *being* and invested in a noema which is correlative to a noesis and cut to its measure. Would it not be necessary, then, in order to make the novelty of the new or the absolute thinkable, to contest this coextension of thought and consciousness in its inter-estedness? Would it not be necessary to put into question the identification of mind with the intellection of being or with the ontology within which the philosophy which has been handed down to us lives?

But what else can one seek than the thought of consciousness and experience, so that, welcoming absolute novelty, it is not stripped of its novelty by its very welcome?

What can come to the knowing mind that is not already contained in it? Are we going to forget Plato's *Meno*? What is this other thought that—neither assimilation nor integration—would not reduce the new to the already known, and would not compromise the novelty of the new by taking its bloom off in the correlation that it sets up? A thought would be necessary that would no longer be constructed as a relation linking the thinker to the thought, or in this thought a relation without correlatives would be necessary, a thought not compelled by the rigorous correspondence between *noesis* and *noema*, not compelled by the adequation of the visible to the aim [*visée*] to which it would respond in the intuition of the truth; a thought would be necessary where the very metaphors of vision and aim would no longer be legitimate.

Impossible exigencies! Unless these exigencies echo what Descartes called the idea-of-the-infinite-in us, thought thinking beyond what it itself contains in the finitude of the cogito, an idea that God, according to Descartes' way of expressing himself, would have deposited in us. This is an exceptional idea, a unique idea, and, for Descartes, the *thinking of God* [*'penser à Dieu'*]. This thinking, in its phenomenology, does not let itself be reduced, without residue, to a subject's act of consciousness, to pure thematizing intentionality. Contrary to the ideas that—though always on the scale of "the intentional object," on the scale of their *ideatum*—are held about it, and contrary to the ideas through which thought progressively grasps the world, the idea of the Infinite would contain more than it could itself contain, more than its *cogito*'s capacity. In some way it would think beyond what it thinks. In its relation to what should be its "intentional" correlate, it would thus be *de-ported*, not culminating, not arriving at an end, at the finish [*à du fini*]. But it is necessary to distinguish between the pure failure of the intentional aim's nonculmination, which would still resort to finality, to the famous teleology of "transcendental consciousness" avowed to a term, on the one hand, and "deportation" or transcendence beyond every end and finality, on the other hand. The latter would be a thought of the absolute without this absolute being reached as an end, which would still signify finality and finitude. The idea of the Infinite must be thought independently from consciousness, not according to the negative concept of the unconscious, but according to the perhaps most profoundly thought thought, that of dis-interestedness, which is a relation without hold on a being, or anticipation of being, but pure patience. This passivity, deference beyond all that is assumed, irreversible de-ference, is time. Would not patience, or the length of time in its dia-chrony—where tomorrow never reaches today—be, prior to all conscious activity—older than consciousness—the most profound thought of the new? Gratuitous like a devotion, this thought would already be misunderstood in its transcendence when one persists in seeking in its dia-chrony and in procrastination, not the surplus—or the Good—of gratuitousness and devotion, but an intentionality, a thematization, and the impatience of a *grasping*.

We think that beyond the apparent negativity of the idea of the Infinite, one can and must find the forgotten horizons of its abstract signification; one must bring the reversal of the teleology of the act of consciousness in dis-inter-ested thought back to the nonfortuitous conditions and circumstances of its signifying in humankind, whose humanity is, perhaps, the putting back into question of the good conscience of being that perseveres in being; and it is advisable to reconstitute the indispensible scenery of the "staging" of this reversal. Such would be the task of a phenomenology of the idea of the Infinite. It did not interest Descartes, for whom the clarity and mathematical distinction of ideas was sufficient, but whose teaching

on the anteriority of the idea of the Infinite in relation to the
idea of the finite is a valuable indication for every phenomenology of consciousness.[10]

We think that the idea-of-the-Infinite-in-me—or my relation to God—comes to me in the concreteness of my relation to the other person, in the sociality which is my
responsibility for the neighbor. This is a responsibility
where, not in any "experience" I have contracted, the face
of the Other, through its alterity, through its very strangeness, speaks the commandment which came *from one knows
not where*. From one knows not where—not as if this face
were an image referring back to an unknown source, to an
inaccessible original, the residue and testimony of a dissimulation, and the last resort of a lost presence, nor as if the
idea of the infinite were the simple negation of every ontological determination one would persist in seeking in its
theoretical essence, suspecting in it, then, the "bad infinite," where it will dissimulate the annoyance of the frus-
trated tendencies of a hidden finality, where an
interminable series of failures is excused, and the impossibility of finishing, opening onto a negative theology, is put
off. Rather, it is as if the face of the other person, which
straightaway "demands of me" and ordains me, were the
node of the very intrigue of God's surpassing of the idea of

[10]Levinas: The formal and paradoxical feature of this idea containing
more than its capacity, and its rupture of the noetic-noematic correlation,
is, to be sure, subordinated in the Cartesian system to the search for a
knowledge. It becomes a link in a proof for the existence of God, who is
thus found to be exposed, as all knowledge correlative to being, to the test
of a suspicious critique, in the surpassing of the given as a transcendental
illusion. Husserl reproaches Descartes for having precipitously acknowl-
edged the soul in the *cogito*, that is, a part of the world, even though the
cogito conditions the world. Likewise, one could contest this reduction of
the problem of God to ontology, as if ontology and knowledge were the
ultimate region of meaning. Does not the extraordinary structure of the
idea of the Infinite, the to-God [*à-Dieu*], signify a spiritual intrigue which
coincides neither with the movement marked by finality, nor with the
auto-identification of identity, such that it de-formalizes itself in self-
consciousness?

God, and of every idea where He would be aimed at, visible, and known, and where the Infinite would be denied through thematization, in presence or representation. It is not in the finality of an intentional aim that I think the infinite. My profoundest thought, which bears all thought, my thought of the infinite older than the thought of the finite,[11] is the very diachrony of time, non-coincidence, dispossession itself: a way of "being avowed" prior to every act of consciousness and more profoundly than consciousness, through the gratuitousness of time (where philosophers have been in fear of vanity or privation). This way of being avowed is devotion. The to-God is precisely not intentionality in its noetic-noematic complexity.

Dia-chrony is a structure that no thematizing and interested movement of consciousness—memory or hope—can either resolve or recuperate in the simultaneities it constitutes. Devotion, in its dis-interestedness, does not lack any end, but is turned around—by a God who in his infinity "loves the stranger"—toward the other person to and for whom I have to respond. Responsibility is without concern for reciprocity: I have to respond to and for the Other without occupying myself with the Other's responsibility in my regard. A relationship without correlation, love of the neighbor is love without eros. It is for-the-other-person and, through this, to-God! Thus thinks a thought which thinks more than it thinks, beyond what it thinks. Demand and responsibility are all the more imperious and urgent as they are undergone with the more patience. The concrete origin or originary situation is where the Infinite is put into me, where the idea of the Infinite commands the mind, and the word God comes to the tip of the tongue. Inspiration is thus the prophetic event of the relation to the new.

---

[11]Levinas: The to-God or the idea of the Infinite, is not a case where intentionality or aspiration would designate the genus. The dynamism of desire refers, to the contrary, to the to-God, a thought profounder and "older" than the cogito.

But also, with the putting into me of the idea of the Infinite, the prophetic event beyond its psychological peculiarity is the throbbing of primordial time where, for itself, of itself, de-formalized, the idea of the Infinite signifies. God-coming-to-mind as the life of God.

Selected Bibliography

La théorie de l'intuition dans la phenoménologie de Husserl (Paris: Alcan, 1930; Paris: Vrin, 1962, 1970, 1984).
  The Theory of Intuition in Husserl's Phenomenology, translated by André Orianne (Evanston: Northwestern, 1973).
De l'évasion (1935) (Montpellier: Fata Morgana, 1982).
De l'existent à l'existence (Paris: Fontaine, 1947; Paris: Vrin, 1973, 1978).
  Existence and Existents, translated by Alphonso Lingis (The Hague: Nijhoff, 1978).
Le temps et l'autre in J. Wahl, *Le Choix, Le Monde, L'Existence* (Grenoble-Paris: Arthaud, 1948), 125–196; with new preface (Montepellier: Fata Morgana, 1979).
  Time and the Other, translated by Richard A. Cohen (Pittsburgh: Duquesne, 1987).
En découvrant l'existence avec Husserl et Heidegger (Paris: Vrin, 1949; 2d ed., 1967, 1974).
Totalité et infini (La Haye, Nijhoff, 1961, 1965, 1968, 1971, 1974, 1980).
  Totality and Infinity, translated by Alphonso Lingis (The Hague: Nijhoff, 1969; Pittsburgh: Duquesne, 1969, 1979).
Difficile liberté (Paris: Albin Michel, 1963; 2d ed., 1976).
Quatre lectures talmudiques (Paris: Minuit, 1968).
Humanisme de l'autre homme (Montpellier: Fata Morgana, 1972).

Autrement qu'être ou au-delà de l'essence (La Haye, Nijhoff, 1974, 1978).
> *Otherwise than Being or Beyond Essence,* translated by Alphonso Lingis (The Hague: Nijhoff, 1981).

Sur Maurice Blanchot (Montpellier: Fata Morgana, 1975).

Noms propres (Montpellier: Fata Morgana, 1975).

Du sacré au saint (Paris: Minuit, 1977).

L'au-delà du verset (Paris: Minuit, 1982).

De Dieu qui vient à l'idée (Paris: Vrin, 1982).

Ethique et infini (Paris: Fayard, 1982).
> *Ethics and Infinity,* translated by Richard A. Cohen (Pittsburgh: Duquesne, 1985).

Transcendance et intelligibilité (Genève: Labor et Fides, 1984).

Collected Philosophical Papers, edited and translated by Alphonso Lingis (The Hague: Nijhoff, 1987).

FORTHCOMING IN ENGLISH:

Discovering Existence with Husserl, edited and translated by Richard A. Cohen (Bloomington: Indiana).

Talmudic Lectures, edited and translated by Annette Aronowitz (Bloomington: Indiana).

SECONDARY IN ENGLISH:

Face to Face with Emmanuel Levinas, edited by Richard A. Cohen (Albany: S.U.N.Y., 1986).

BIBLIOGRAPHY

Emmanuel Levinas: Une bibliographie primaire et secondaire (1929-1985) by Roger Burggraeve (Leuven: Peeters, 1986). To obtain, write: Center for Metaphysics and Philosophy of God, Institute of Philosophy, Kardinaal Mercier-plein 2, 3000 Leuven, Belgium.

Index

Index

Abraham, 24
Allison, David, 47n.
Aminadab (Blanchot), 56, 83
Anaximander, 108
Anonymity, 47, 48, 51, 52
Aristophanes, 86n.
Aristotle, 43n., 49n., 119, 129
Athens and Jerusalem (Shestov), 76n.
Augustine, 115
Auschwitz, 26
Authority, 106, 114, 117
Autre, viii, 30n.
Autre homme, viii, 30n.
Autrui, viii, 30n.

"Bad Conscience and the Inexorable" (Levinas), 73n.
Batailles, Georges, 47n.
Beavoir, Simone de, 85n.
Befindlichkeit, 116
Being and Nothingness (Sartre), 56n., 87n., 93n.
Being and Time (Heidegger), 7, 40, 44, 49n., 51n., 56n., 59n., 60n., 62n., 70n., 99, 115, 118n., 130n.
Bergson, Henri, 5, 11, 12, 34, 47n., 53, 76, 80, 91, 119, 122, 125n., 128, 130-133
Besorgen, 62n.
Beyond Good and Evil (Nietzsche), 47n.
Bible, 83n., 119
Blanchot, Maurice, 56, 83
Bloy, Leon, 86

Briefe and Tagebucher (Rosenzweig), 121
Brock, Werner, 49n.
Buber, Martin, 93, 94n.

Cambodia, 26
Camus, Albert, 50n.
Caress, 89
Cartesian Meditations (Husserl), 75n.
Chalier, Catherine, 85n.
Chesed, 84n.
Child, 91
Civilization, 82, 84
Cogito, 99, 101, 125, 134, 136n., 137n.
Cohen, Richard, 45n., 64n., 73n., 84n., 87n.
Collected Philosophical Papers of Emmanuel Levinas, The, (Levinas), 33n.
Command, 106, 113, 136
Communion, 93, 94
Conatus essendi, 109, 112, 121
Conscience, 27, 109, 110, 114, 117, 118
Consciousness, 51, 88, 97, 130, 133-135
Cratylus, 49
Creative Evolution (Bergson), 119, 120
Creative Mind, The, (Bergson), 76n., 131n., 132n.
Crisis of European Sciences and Transcendental Phenomenology, The, (Husserl), 98

Critique of Pure Reason (Kant), 46n.
Crusoe, Robinson, 43

Dante, Alighieri, 86
Dasein, 8, 16, 40, 44n., 59n., 62n., 70, 93, 99, 110, 115
"De l'evasion" (Levinas), 71n.
Death, 8, 9, 41, 69-74, 76-79, 81, 90, 92, 114-116
Deformalization, 119, 136n.
Deleuze, Gilles 47n.
Deliberation, 111, 113
Descartes, Rene, 23, 99, 117, 125, 134-136n.
Derrida, Jacques, 3, 15, 20-22, 44n.
Devotion, 137
Diachrony, 22, 112, 113, 118, 135, 137
Dialectic, 100
Dialogue, 100
Dire, 103
Dis-inter-est, 135, 137
Dit, 103
Dostoyevsky, Fyodor, 108
Duration, 80, 81, 129, 130, 132
Durkheim, Emile, 84, 93n.

Economics, 61
Ecstasis, 6, 7
Egology, 98, 100, 101, 114
Eigentlichkeit, 44n.
Élan vital, 91, 119
Eleatic, 91, 92
Election, 108
Emphasis, 22, 25
Enjoyment, 63, 67
Epicurus, 71n.
Eros, 10, 76, 88, 90, 91, 137
Esau, 61
Esse, 109
Eternity, 49, 111
Ethics, 14-18

Ethics and Infinity (Levinas), 85n.
Evil, 51
Existence and Being (Heidegger), 49n.
Existence and Existents (Levinas), 2-4, 6, 42n., 46n., 48n., 50n., 51n., 55n., 64n., 66n., 76n., 82n.
Expression, 20, 107

Face, 18, 19, 105, 107, 113
Face-to-Face, 78, 79
Face-to-Face with Levinas (Cohen, ed.), 73n., 84n., 87n.
Fecundity, 37, 91, 92
Feminine, 36, 85-88
Figures du féminin (Chalier), 85n.
Freedom, 54-57, 62, 87, 124, 125
Freud, Sigmund, 47n., 89, 90
Fürsorge, 62n.
Future, 10, 22, 76, 77, 79, 82, 88-90, 94, 115, 116, 119, 130

Gegebenheit, 98
Gevurah, 84n.
Geworfenheit, 45, 119, 132
Glatzer, Nahum, 46n.
God, 4, 19, 23, 24, 30, 31, 44, 45n., 114-118, 120, 125, 134, 136-138
"God and Philosophy" (Levinas), 33n., 51n.
God Who Comes to the Idea (Levinas), 3, 4
Goethe, Johann Wolfgang von, 86
Goodness, 16, 32, 117, 135
Goulag, 26
Greisch, Jean, viii

Hamlet, 73n., 78
Hamlet (Shakespeare), 73
Hayyim of Volozhyn, 23, 24
Hegel, George Wilhelm
    Friedrich, 1, 2, 12, 42, 46n.,
    87, 122, 126-128
Heidegger, Martin, 6-8, 10, 11,
    13, 16, 21, 29n., 34, 40, 41,
    44, 45, 49, 51, 56n., 59,
    60n., 62, 63, 68, 70, 71n.,
    75n., 76n., 93, 99, 109, 116,
    118n., 119, 128, 132, 133
Heraclitus, 49
Hersch, Jeanne, 29
Heteronomy, 114
Hiroshima, 26
Hitler, Adolf, 26, 47n.
Holocaust, 120
Holzwege (Heidegger), 109
Hope, 73
Hostage, 108
How Natives Think
    (Levy-Bruhl), 93n.
Husserl, Edmund, 2, 5, 11,
    13, 20, 34, 60n., 64n., 75n.,
    98, 99, 102, 131n., 136n.
Husserlian Meditations
    (Sokolowski), 60n.
Hypostasis, 43, 51, 52

Idealism, 46, 60, 68, 116
"Il y a" (Levinas), 46n.
Infinite, 117, 118, 134-138
Insomnia, 48
Inspiration, 137
Instant, 5
Intentionality, 97, 98, 102, 114,
    134, 136n.
Intuition, 130, 131, 133
Irigaray, Luce, 84n.

Jacob, 61
Jankelevitch, Vladimir, 34, 35,
    73n.

Jaspers, Karl, 29n.
Jemeinigkeit, 45, 99, 115
Jouissance, 63
Joyce, James, 15
Justice, 104, 106-108, 118

Kant, Immanual, 46, 53, 99,
    118n.
Kaufmann, Walter, 47n.
Kearney, Richard, 87n.
Khersonsky, N., 11
Kierkegaard, Søren, 59

Language, 21, 99
"Letter on Humanism"
    (Heidegger), 60n.
Letter to Menoeceus (Epicurus),
    71
Letters to his Fiancée (Bloy), 86
Levy-Bruhl, Lucien, 42, 93n.
Libido, 89
*Libido: The French Existential
    Theories* (Lingis), 84n.
Light, 64-66
Lingis, Alphonso, 33n., 47n.,
    65n., 74n., 84n.
Logical Investigations (Husserl),
    98
Love, 88, 108, 110, 116, 120,
    137
Lucretius, 78

Macbeth, 50, 72, 73
Macduff, 72, 73
Marcel, Gabriel, 34
Marx, Karl, 47n., 79
Mastery, 74, 87
Mauss, Marcel, 93n.
Même, viii
Meno (Plato), 134
Merleau-Ponty, Maurice, 29n.,
    34, 60n.

Metaphysical Journal (Marcel),
    34
Metaphysics (Aristotle), 49n.
Materiality, 56-58, 62, 67
Matter and Memory (Bergson),
    119
Miteinandersein, 40, 93
Mitsein, 75n.
Modernity, 99, 124-126
Mortality, 107
Mystery, 33, 41, 70, 75
Myth of Sisyphus, The,
    (Camus), 50n.

Nature of Sympathy, The,
    (Scheler), 75n.
Nausea (Sartre), 71n.
Nefesh Hahayyim, (Hayyim of
    Volozhyn), 23, 24
Negation, 12, 32, 33n., 48, 73
Nemo, Philippe, 37n.
New, 121, 123, 127, 128, 131,
    133, 137
New Nietzsche, The, (Allison,
    ed.), 47n.
Nietzsche, Friedrich, 47n., 59,
    128
Nietzsche and Philosophy
    (Deleuze), 47n.
Noema, 18, 53n., 98, 108, 134
Noesis, 18, 53n., 98, 134
Non-in-difference, 13, 108,
    115, 116, 118
Noms Propre (Levinas), 94n.

O'Conner, D. J., 43n.
Odysseus, 24
Old, 122-124, 127
*Otherwise than Being or Beyond
    Essence* (Levinas), 3, 4, 10,
    20, 21, 33n., 64n., 65n.,
    104n., 112n.
Ousia, 43n.

Parmenides, 42, 43, 45n.,
    47n., 85

Pascal, Blaise, 24, 59, 78,
    112n.
Passivity, 17, 73, 112
Past, 22, 82, 102, 111-113, 118,
    119, 123, 130
Paternity, 36, 91, 92
Patience, 135
Pfeiffer, Gabrielle, 75n.
Phenomenology, 1, 35, 89, 92,
    109, 135
*Phenomenology of Internal
    Time-Consciousness, The,*
    (Husserl), 60n.
Phenomenology of Perception
    (Merleau-Ponty), 60n.
Phenomenology of Spirit
    (Hegel), 47n.
Philosophies Premiere
    (Jankelevitch), 73n.
Philosophies of Existence (Wahl),
    34n.
Philosophy, 58, 126, 127, 132
Philosophy of Martin Buber, The,
    (Schillp and Friedman,
    eds.), 94n.
Plato, 14, 64n., 86n., 92-94,
    100, 129, 134
Platonism, 64n., 76, 84, 91
Plotinus, 44n.
Present, 52-54, 122
Presocratic Philosophers, The,
    (Kirk, Raven, and Schofield,
    eds.), 49n.
Prophetic event, 137, 138
Proximity, 32, 94, 104, 108
Pygmalion, 81

Quiddity, 130n.

Reason, 65, 66, 97, 101
Reciprocity, 83, 93, 108
Religion, 32, 120
Representation, 11, 101, 103,
    106, 113, 118
Responsibility, 25, 72, 104,
    108, 110-115, 136, 137

Revelation, 24, 115, 119
Ricoeur, Paul, 126
Rolland, Jacques, viii, 10, 71n.
Romeo and Juliette
(Shakespeare), 50
Rosenzweig, Franz, 23, 45n.,
46n., 76n., 110n., 119, 121n.

Salvation, 61
Sartre, Jean-Paul, 34, 56n., 62,
71n., 76, 87n., 93n.
Saying, 21, 22, 103
Scheler, Max, 75n.
Science, 44, 125-127, 133
Second Sex, The, (Beauvoir),
85n.
Seeing, 97-99
Sein-zum-Tode, 119
Sex, 36, 85, 86, 92
Shakespeare, William, 50n.,
59, 72
Shestov, Lev, 76n.
*Short History of Existentialism,
A,* (Wahl), 87n.
Sinngebung, 115
Sleep, 49, 51
Socialism, 59, 61
Solitude, 40, 42, 43, 54, 55,
59, 59, 65, 74, 77
Sokolowski, Robert, 60n.
Sorge, 62n.
Stalin, Joseph, 26
Star of Redemption, The,
(Rosenzweig), 23, 45n.,
46n., 76n., 110n.
State, 105
Stoekl, Allan, 47n.
Substantia, 43n.
Suffering, 68, 69, 72
Suicide, 50
Symposium (Plato), 86n.

There is, 46, 48, 50, 51
Third person, 106

Time, 6, 30, 31, 39, 92, 102,
115, 119, 122, 123, 126, 127,
131, 137, 138
Time and Free Will (Bergson),
119, 125n.
Time and the Other (Levinas),
71n., 73n., 85n., 87n.
To-God, 23, 24, 118, 120, 137
Tools, 62, 63, 68
Totalitarianism, 26
Totality and Infinity (Levinas),
3, 4, 9, 10, 12, 13, 15, 17, 18,
20, 21, 23, 30n., 42n., 46n.,
49n., 50n., 53n., 55n., 64n.,
66n., 68n., 70n., 71n., 74n.,
75n., 82n.-84n.
Trace, 19
Tragedy, 40, 50, 57, 59, 72
*Two Sources of Morality and
Religion, The,* (Bergson), 119,
120

*Understanding the Sick and the
Healthy* (Rosenzweig), 46n.

Urimpression, 5

Visions of Excess (Bataille), 47n.
Voluptuousness, 10, 89, 90

Waelhens, Alphonse de, 64n.
Wahl, Jean, 29, 30n., 33, 34,
46, 70n., 87n.
Wahl, Marcelle, 30n.
Wenzler, Ludwig, viii, ix
"What is Metaphysics"
(Heidegger), 49n.
Will to Power, 47n.
Will to Power, The, (Nietzsche),
47n.
Work, 68
Writing and Difference
(Derrida), 44n.

Youth, 130